Gloves

by Ernie Farrar
and
Alan E. Rubel

Edited by Robert Winkler, University of Vermont

Vermont Golden Gloves
Amateur Boxing in Vermont

D1595854

First printed in 2008.

Published by Alan E. Rubel
56 Ayers Street
Barre, Vermont 05641

Printed in the State of Vermont, United States of America.

For general information contact:

Alan E. Rubel
56 Ayers Street
Barre, Vermont 05641
802-476-3063
802-479-1866 Fax
alan.rubel@proforma.com

Dedication

This book is dedicated to my family. Children, David Rubel and his wife Minori, Erica McNamara and her husband Kevin, Robert Vandor and his wife Jill, David Vandor and his wife Laynie, and Michael Vandor. Our twelve extraordinary grandchildren, Lia, Noah, Sara, Jaye, Lisa, Kieran, Kaitlyn, Lucy, Cole, Elizabeth, Sarah and Tommy. My parents Ben and Rose Rubel. To my soulmate Sharon for her patience, support and guidance over the last two years.

And to a champion, childhood hero, who's inspiration, has guided the writing of this book, my friend Firpo.

May you rest in peace.

Alan E. Rubel

I would like to dedicate "Gloves" to my wife Sherry and our off-spring, Tony and wife Heather, Michael, Amy, Becky, Rachel, grandchildren Brandon, and Erika. They have all assisted in making the Vermont Golden Gloves Tournament a success. Also, to my good friends the late Jimmy Sheridan and Bernie Cummings as well as all the boxers who participated in the "Golden Gloves" through the years.

Ernie Farrar

Acknowledgements

We would like to acknowledge Con Hogan for all his guidance and wisdom. Our Editor, Robert Winkler, for the extraordinary job he has done. Mona Arruda for all the extra work and direction she has given us. Tom Davis for all his help. To the staff of Friendly's Restaurant in Colchester who put up with our fun and laughter during our meetings as we worked on "Gloves" for the last two years.

And to many people who have helped in the writing of "Gloves".

Preface

The book "Gloves" is a compilation of short and sometimes long stories of boxers not only from the state of Vermont but the entire region. It took a lot of research to put the book together and the purpose is to bring back memories and recognize some of the people who brought excitement to the sport. This is an "open ended" book which means the book will be updated with new faces and additional information in the future. We realize people will ask "why is so and so not in the book" he/she was a champion "Glover". With your input, names, years they boxed, photos and clippings they too can be included in the book as well. "Gloves" has been in the works, off and on for two years, again, it took a lot of research and we want to thank regional boxing historian, Bob Winkler, of the University of Vermont for all the work he has done to make the book possible. The authors, Ernie Farrar and Alan Rubel, are not writers but did their very best putting pen to paper! We hope you enjoy "Gloves".

Table of Contents

Chapter One

An Early History of Boxing in Vermont
Howard Opera House, Burlington (1879-1904)

Listen to the Voices
A Historical Snapshot of Boxing in Vermont
by Bob Winkler

Boxing can be traced in the United States, and no less so in Vermont, to the time of the American Revolution and has gone through ebbs and flows in popularity ever since. Indeed, pugilist venues were many times mere brawls, commonly set up in fields as far away from the police as possible, and many times resulted in injurious behavior on the part of its participants and onlookers. Many American states and Canadian provinces outlawed boxing exhibitions at various times in their history. Boxing parlors were common for the rich and influential though, and amateur boxing matches were very popular with college men, clergymen and at area military camps. Vermont displayed a particularly straight-laced citizenry at times outlawing, or attempting to outlaw, touring musical troupes at town meeting halls and public gatherings. So, when the Howard Opera House opened in Burlington, Vermont, in 1879, its owner John Purple Howard had to make assurances that the performances were of high caliber and thus opera houses came to occupy the landscape throughout the length and breadth of Vermont. Still by the 1890s Operatic Burlesque, wrestling, vaudeville and prizefighting became common fare.* When the Howard Opera House closed in November, 1904, it was soon replaced by the Strong Theatre in Burlington, and if we listen hard enough we can hear those voices from the past.

Bellows Falls, Vermont
Young Sidney, by clever head work, won the decision over Jack Hamilton in a fifteen round bout before the Fall Mountain Athletic Club last night.
Bennington Evening Banner, October 8, 1904

Brattleboro, Vermont
Jack Clune, boxing promoter, is in communication with George M. Lawrence of New York relative to putting on an exhibition 10-round bout in Brattleboro by Sam McVea, the colored marvel, and his boxing partner, Bob Devere. Mr. Clune realizes that this is something of an undertaking, but he wants to give the fans a top-liner that they will always remember and he purposes to make a canvass to see what the prospects are for supporting such an exceptional attraction.

McVea has knocked out almost every white fighter he has met and has defeated the four greatest colored men in his class namely, Sam Langford, Joe Jeanette, "Battling" Jim Johnson and Harry "The Black Panther" Wills. For the past six years he has been the greatest fighter attraction in the business.

Devere is an Irishman twenty years old, six feet tall and weighs 198 pounds. He has had twenty-one fights, out of which he has knocked out seventeen men and received the referees decision twice. He has knocked out Sailor Grande, Marty Cutler–trainer of Jack Johnson, Jack Lester, Jim McCormack, Dick Lawless and others. The Irish giant is ready to meet any heavyweight boxer in the world.

Brattleboro Daily Reformer, January 4, 1916

Memorial Auditorium, Burlington, Vermont

Micky "Kid" Williams defeated Young "Iron Man" Goulette for the state welterweight title in an eight round semi-final at the new auditorium last night before a thousand boxing fans. Williams and Goulette went at it apache fashion and kept Jack Barrett on the jump throughout the eight rounds. The two lads swung punches from everywhere in Europe and back again, and strange to say most of them landed. If Williams shoulders had been at all sensitive, he would have taken the count, for Goulette hammered away at the shoulders until they were worn red. Then in the sixth frame, Williams five times sent mighty lefts to the Iron Man's jaw shaking him to the foundation, but Goulette merely shook them off and staggered in for more. Two judges offered Williams [the decision] and the crowd booed for five minutes. However, it must be acknowledged that it was a different Williams in the ring last night. Dropping his role of clown, he got down to business, fought earnestly and proved himself a fine sportsman.

Burlington Free Press and Times, June 2, 1928

Union Street Auditorium, Bennington, Vermont
Sylvester Davis KOs Kid Jack in 3

In round one, Kid Jack lost his head because Davis failed to break when the referee said to, he became angered and forgot some of the rules of the ring. In the second round, Kid Jack loses his temper, and is completely cutboxed by Davis. In the third round, Davis hits Kids breadbasket and then lands a left to the mouth, at which point, Kid Jack goes down for an eight count before the towel is finally heaved in by the seconds.

Bennington Evening Banner, October 19, 1934

Granite Street Hall, Barre, Vermont
Jack Reno with a Decision in 8 Over Bobby Simpson

Reno is a wild southpaw and his unorthodox stance bothered the New Hampshire boxer. There were very few heavy blows during the eight rounds. Reno relied on slaps to the ribs and a rabbit punch, that should have brought disqualification, but coupled with his aggressiveness, it brought him a win. Simpson showed some clean boxing ability and cut some nice hooks to Reno's mid-riff, but he did not crowd in enough to take the award. There were no knockdowns.

**From "In The Forests" byline, 1217th Company, CCC Ricker Mills.*

Jack Reno, a member of this camp and former amateur lightweight champion of New Jersey, remained undefeated after his thirteen fight in Vermont when he handed his latest opponent, Bobby Simpson, an artistic lacing in eight rounds at the Granite Street Hall in Barre. This match featured an evening of glove slinging in which enrollees of the 1217th held the spotlight.

Barre Daily Times, May 10 & 14, 1935

---

*George B. Bryan, The Howard Opera House in Burlington, Vermont History 45 (1977) 197-220.

A Bit of History

In the 1920's, 30's & 40's, Vermont was a hotbed of boxing. Bouts were held in various cities and towns in the state including Burlington's Woodman Hall, Bennington's Hawk Auditorium on Union Street, Barre's Granite Street Hall, the Northfield Armory, and the Lamoille Valley Fair in Morrisville, the Champlain Valley Exposition in Essex Jct., Hardwick and the Newport Armory on Main Street. Other locations and participants came from the Concurrent Military Training Camp, Colchester, the Waterbury and Peru C.C.C. Camps and the Meadow Brook Arena in North Adams, Massachusetts. If you lived in the Newport area, boxing could also be found in Stanstead and Sherbrooke, Quebec.

Growing up in Newport, I never heard much about boxing or what a hot bed it was for the sport. Since leaving the area many years ago, I'm now just finding out how popular the sport was and who some of the pugilists were from the area. I never knew my brother-in-law, Alfred Monfette and his brothers Joe and Pete were boxers! Alfred never mentioned he boxed in the Armory on Main Street. There were many other boxers from that era as well: Jesse Cartee, (aka Hub Parker), Tony Marandola (aka Tony Marondo) Victor Carter, Jr. (aka "Bombshell" Carter). There was also Elwood Smith of Coventry, Earl Tarbox of Orleans, Gaston LaMarche and Forest Lafoe of Orleans, Zeke Cushing from North Troy and Charley Conley of Sheffield. These were just a few of the boxers that come to mind at this time, of course, there were others.

The three boxers that come to mind are Hub Parker, Tony Marondo (he was known as Two-Bee Marondo in Newport) and "Bombshell" Carter. Growing up in Newport and living in various places, I got to know these three but they never talked boxing. Hub Parker, Vermont Middleweight Champion, was my neighbor on Hill Street. We lived over, what was Kendall's Market, at the time, and Hub and his family lived across the hall from us. I always knew him as a house painter and not a boxer but he was one hell of a middleweight boxer. Then living "around the bend" as we would say, or as everyone called it "Skunk Hollow", my neighbors were the Carter family. Victor, Sr., and his wife, Helen, had a large family. I was a little kid and would go play with their grandson, Leo Judd, or as we called him "Junior". In the Carter family living room hung a picture of lightweight champion "Bombshell" in a boxing pose. I never knew much about Victor, Jr., until the latter years but he was excellent in the ring and boxed his way to a New England Championship. Then, moving to Glen Road, a section of Newport known at the time as "Little Chicago" or "Chiefo". I've even heard it referred to as "Stovepipe City". Yes, as you can imagine from the nicknames, it was a rough area in the early years. The Cheney twins, Edgar and Irwin, lived in that area. They were fighters both in and outside the ring. I'm not knocking them as they were good people, but they did like to "rough-house" it once in a while! Living off a side street from Glen Road, either Fairview or Hinman, was the Marandola family. Tony or Two-Bee, as we called him, not only boxed in the Newport area but in various other parts of the country and at one time lived in the northwest part of the United States. He was one tough boxer. My friend the late Mahlon Steinhour, of St. Albans, could attest to that. Mahlon was also an excellent boxer himself. Knowing I once lived in Newport he said he boxed a guy from that area. "His name was Tony Marandola and he was a tough son-of-a-gun," said Mahlon. How did you do? Steinhour said, "He beat the hell out of me!" As a kid I used to go fishing for perch on the "Long Bridge" with TwoBee. We always talked about fishing and never about boxing. Never knew he boxed. He liked to smoke cigars and if the fishing was slow, he would hand me money, and send me off to the neighborhood store to get him a pack of Dexter Cigars and a soda for me. I'll always remember that. Two-Bee's nephew, Donald Lontine, boxed in the Vermont Golden Gloves in the mid 1950's. He went the distance with "Cowboy" Lewis, losing on a decision.

Thanks to Hub Parker's son, Ken Cartee, I was able to get an insight into some of the boxing matches his father was involved in. Information was difficult to find and Ken so graciously loaned me his scrapbook of clippings about his father and other boxers who fought in the Northeast Kingdom.

Snip-Its From The Clippins'
Hub Parker Wins by K.O. In Barre

Fight fans 600 strong jammed the Barre armory for the first boxing show there in five years. Hub Parker of Newport, retained his Vermont middleweight crown in the main event knocking out "K.O." Spindolini of New Britain, Connecticut, in the eighth round. It was billed for 10 rounds.

In the semi-final bout, Charlie Beaupre of Burlington, had his hands full to retain his Welterweight crown. Beaupre pulled out a draw with Jackie Fournier of Beebe, Quebec.

Newport Daily Express

Ray Teja Wins Decision from Parker

Ray Teja of East Barre, swooped down on Hub Parker of Newport in the ten round main event of the Firpo-Alywood Boxing Show at the Barre Armory last night. When it was over, Teja not only walked off with the decision, but the full purse (winner-take-all) and the middleweight title of the state. From the fourth round on, it was Teja's fight. Parker went down four times for the count of nine, he went through the ropes and became entangled in the ropes several times. All the while Teja was displaying some classy in-fighting. He went to work on Parker's head and body, mostly his head, firing fast shots, fast blows with both guns. The winner and new champ, Ray Teja, will meet Don Labbe of Lewiston, Maine, in the near future.

Buster Beaupre of Burlington and Johnny Stewart of Berlin went to an eight round draw in the best scrap of the show.

Announcement was made that Charlie Conley of Glover will meet K.O. Clough of Washington, Vermont, on the next show.

Newport Daily Express

Much Interest In Local Boxing Card

Jack Fournier, Hub Parker, Freddie Prue, Tony Marondo, and "Bombshell" Carter Headline Fine Program Monday in the Newport Armory. In the main event of the evening, Jack Fournier of Beebe and Lou Forkas of Fort Ethan Allen will headline the 26 round card.

In the semi-final go of six rounds, popular "Hub" Parker, who claims to be in the best physical condition of his career, will step it out with the Fort Ethan Allen Middleweight Champion Joe Sprano. Parker surprised everyone by knocking out Spindolini at Barre three weeks ago to retain his state title and last week he knocked K.O. Kasper into a frigid state at Barre. Sprano, in the same stable as Spindolini is anxious to tackle the blonde mitt man and has confidence of taking up where Spindolini stopped and whip the Newport boy.

One of the most interesting bouts on the card will be the four round prelim between "Bombshell" Carter and "Machine Gun" Mike Malshuk of Orleans, although two other four rounders with Tony Marondo of Newport vs Nick Stark of Hardwick and Freddie Prue of Newport vs Stan Michaels of Fort Ethan Allen, hold plenty of interest. Most of the fans will have their attention focused on Prue, who looms as the best up-and-coming fighter Newport has seen in a long time.

Newport Daily Express

Seven Hundred See Fournier, Parker Win Top Events

700 boxing fans witnessed five knock outs on a card of an equal number of bouts at the Newport Armory last night. With the exception of young "Vic" Carter, who had the towel tossed in on him in the first heat of his bout with Billy Malshuk of Orleans, the local pugilists went to town. "Tony" Marondo kayoed "Nick" Stark of Hardwick in the second round. "Freddie" Prue sent Stan Michaels of Fort Ethan Allen to slumberland in the first frame, "Hub" Parker did the same kind of job on "Joe" Sprano from the post and in the main event "Lou" Forkas stuck it out for four rounds against "Jackie" Fournier, the Beebe Bomber.

The standout local performer was "Freddie" Prue. Freddie landed the hardest wallop of the whole show when he clipped Michaels with his dynamite left mitt in the opening session of the third prelim scheduled for four rounds. Prue in the short time he was in the roped off arena, gave every indication of a real comer.

Newport Daily Express

Midget Boxing Twins

Edgar and Irwin, nine years of age, twin sons of Mr. and Mrs. Leo Cheney, Glen Road, introduced as the only twins of their weight, fighting in New England opened the boxing matches at the Newport Armory last night with three one minute rounds. Even though brothers, they did not spare each other and displayed the science of professionals.

They tipped the scales under the half hundred mark and were surprisingly clever and hit plenty hard. They had the audience in an uproar, and the crowd showered the mat with silver after the last round.

Their tiny hands were not equal to the shower and grown-ups assisted them in gathering money that fell like rain.

They were so well matched that they received a judges decision of a draw. A checkup of the money received from the audience revealed $11.62. Gilly Vanier acted as referee.

In the three/four round prelims "Tony" Marondo, the local Italian, kept up his kayo record by sending "Bob" Robitaille of Derby and South Troy to dreamland in the first heat. "Little Mike" Malshuk of Orleans scored a kayo over Newport's "Wild Bill" Beck in the third round after the latter had put up a game fight for two rounds. The "Vic" Carter vs Art Laplante bout went the distance with the inexperienced West Sider standing up under "Bombshell" Carters barrage of blows. Carter held a wide margin on points to take the decision. Vic weighed 109, while Laplante weighed 114.

The semi-final bout was a free-for-all between Newport's "Hub" Parker and Leo Langevin of Sherbrooke. Langevin the 42 year old ring veteran, who has seen over two hundred ring battles was far too clever for the local boy, but points which Parker piled up on left jabbing won for him the decision which was very unpopular.

The main event was a thriller from the outset. "Buster" Beaupre of Burlington weighing 135, held the upper hand for the greater part of the mill, but Canadian Petit, 136, staged a real comeback in the eighth chapter to give the bout that certain something that left much doubt in the minds of the fans as to which was the better man. According to tabulations, the first round was even, Beaupre took the next three, the fifth was even, Petit won the sixth, the seventh went to the Burlington boy and Petit held a wide edge in the last round. The decision in favor of Beaupre met with wide approval.

Newport Daily Express

Maine's Labbe Cops Decision

Had Newport's "Hub" Parker kept up his first round style of boxing, he might have stolen the decision from Lewiston, Maine's Don Labbe in the evenings feature event at the armory. Parker, 158, piled up the points in the opening session with his left jabbing, keeping the Maine boy, 155, at a safe distance, but in the second round and throughout the remainder of the mill the local boy dropped his left and left himself open with Labbe working in on fast spurts to register effective blows with hard lefts. Only once after the first round did Parker use his left to any great advantage and that was in the third stanza. According to the writers tabulation, Parker won the first and third rounds, Labbe took the second, the fourth was even and Labbe carried the last four rounds.

Never knew where area boxers trained for upcoming matches or who managed the boxers and worked their corners. I'm told that Frank Carbonneau of Newport, would move all the furniture and train boxers in his living room. I believe he had a son, Donald, that boxed.

There were other boxers from the Newport area besides the above mentioned: Arland "Josh" Hall won the novice division of the Vermont Golden Gloves in the 160 lb class in the early 1960's. Hall, a Marine, went on to have a successful pro career in the light heavyweight division. He resides in the Baltimore, Maryland, area where he is a trainer and has a gym full of boxers. John Hurlbut, who worked at Montgomery Wards and later managed a bowling alley, boxed in the gloves in the mid 50's. Dr. Dennis LeBlanc, a dentist, with a practice in Derby, boxed and was later appointed to the Vermont Boxing Control Board. There were others, Roland Britch, who boxed in the Golden Gloves in the early years. Bat Martineau, Kit Britch, Joe Rushlow all from Newport. There was also "Kid" Morrisette from Island Pond and, of course, there was also the "Flying Auger" Brothers from the Newport Center area who boxed in the gloves. They were trapeze artists who would entertain at local fairs.

The southern part of Vermont was also a hot bed of boxing. Bob Winkler, who has worked on this book, is a boxing historian. Check out his website esfuvm.edu/vtbox and find out more about boxing in the state. Find out how Emil Dupre, "Battlin" Fitz, Armand "Kid" Cioffi, "Cowboy", Gaudreau, Gerald Markey, Moe Ladue, Leo Berard, "Kid" Chaples, K.O. Kaspar and others faired in the ring.

Newport Daily Express

Hub Parker (Jesse Cartee–real name).

Historical Timeline

The Newport, Vermont, area was a hotbed of boxing in the 1930's and 40's. Here is information from a poster, courtesy of Bruce Smith of Derby. He found the poster in his late father Elwood's scrapbook. We were unable to make a copy the poster.

LAST SHOW OF THE SEASON
THURSDAY JUNE 22, 1937

6 RD

ELWOOD SMITH VS CHARLIE CONLEY
COVENTRY   SHEFFIELD

FRED PRUE VS WESLEY MERCIER
NEWPORT   HARDWICK

GASTON LaMARCHE VS FOREST LAFOE
ORLEANS   ORLEANS

JOE MOFFETT VS DICK DAVIS
NEWPORT   ISLAND POND

MIKE MALSHUK VS ZEKE CUSHING
ORLEANS   NO. TROY

EARL TARBOX VS ALFRED MONFETTE
ORLEANS   NEWPORT

HELD AT NEWPORT ARMORY

CONLEY HAS BEATEN ALL HIS OPPONENTS ...
SMITH SAYS HE'LL TAKE
HIM TO CAMP LIKE HE HAS OTHERS

PROMOTER, LITTLE JOE CRUSO

ADDMISSION 55 cents STUDENTS 25 cents
RESERVED 85 cents

Courtesy of Bruce Smith of Derby.

The Summer of '34
"History Worth Repeating"
by Bob Winkler

In the summer of 1934, the world was moving along at a fast pace. John Dillinger, the Desperado, was slain–Babe Ruth hit his 699th home run–Hitler's troops took over Austria–thousands went to Plymouth, Vermont, to pay tribute to the late President Calvin Coolidge–and there was snow in Vermont on August 6th.

In the world of boxing, the likes of Joe Louis [who would become heavyweight champion of the world in 1937], Max Baer [who trained in Speculator, New York], and King Levinsky filled the front pages. Vermont boxing, meanwhile, was relegated to the sports page of area newspapers like the Bennington Evening Banner and the Burlington Free Press and Times.

Summer affairs such as the annual Danville Fair, the Lamoille Valley Fair in Morrisville, the Northfield Armory, and the Champlain Valley Exposition in Essex Junction–held many popular boxing events, where local favorites where challenged by pugilists from New York, Massachusetts, New Hampshire, Maine and Canada.

The Champlain Valley Exposition boxing card was particularly brilliant that year. The event held during the last day of the fair on the evening of September 1st, featured 28 rounds of exciting boxing viewed by a crowd of over 800. Seven Vermont lads came away with an impressive showing of three wins, three draws, and only one defeat.

Gerald Markey of Burlington, a lightweight at 130 lbs was featured in the main event of 8 rounds against Frankie "Young" Weiss of Albany, New York–weighing in at 134 lbs. Markey went on to win a decision in eight.

The first semi-final bout pitted Mike Davies of Burlington–a last minute substitution for "Rocky" Homer, the colored tornado who had just moved up from Boston against Freddie Sexton of Glens Falls, New York. Despite the fifteen pounds weight difference, they went the full 6 rounds for a draw. King Phillips of St. Albans was featured in the second semi-final bout with a 4th round TKO over Tommy Murphy of Albany, New York.

In the first of two preliminary bouts, "Young" Bissette of Burlington fought to a 4th round draw with "Kid" Fay of Lakeside [Burlington]. Johnny House of Winooski won a 4th round decision in the 150 lb class against fellow Vermonter, Billy Robinson of Burlington.

Meanwhile, in the southern part of the state, Emil Dupre of Danby, Vermont, middleweight, was down at the Meadow Brook Arena in North Adams, Massachusetts–getting an early start to his fight season by going the distance in a four round decision given Eddie the "Pride of the Berkshires" Decker of Housatonic, Massachusetts, on the evening of August 23rd. Emil would go on to compile a one win, and three loss record, all by decisions, at the V.F.W. sponsored fight cards at the Union Street Auditorium in Bennington. He would register a 4th round decision against Charlie Shea of Athol, Massachusetts, on October 18th, and would go on to have three 4th round decisions against him by Johnny McCarty of Worcester, Massachusetts, on November 1st, and twice by "Wild" Freddie Wright–Bennington's "Rising Star"–on February 15th and 28th.

Noteworthy news events of the day recorded in the Bennington Banner where the opening of Bennington College [a women's college] for it's third year, the cruise ship "Morro Castle" catching fire off the New Jersey coast, and Bing Crosby, Miriam Hopkins and Kitty Carlisle appearing for two days at the General Stark Theatre in Bennington.

Ferdinand "Young Firpo" Saldi
Barre, Vermont
Boxer, Trainer/Coach, Promoter Extraordinaire
June 4, 1910 - December 29, 1981

Firpo was an area businessman, community leader, entrepreneur, boxing champion, manager and promoter. He started Firpo's Restaurant in the 1940s, and later Howard Johnsons Restaurant in 1949 on the Barre-Montpelier Road in Berlin, Vermont. He also owned a granite quarry.

He was co-founder of Community Services, a non-profit that built Skyline Ski area, and worked with youth in the greater Barre area.

Firpo started boxing at the age of sixteen under the name of Young Firpo, and became one of the greatest fighters to ever come out of Vermont. He was Vermont's lightweight and welterweight champion with a record of sixty-three wins and three defeats. One of the losses was against the great world lightweight champion by the name of Benny Leonard who some say was pound-for-pound one of the greatest fighters that ever lived! Early in his boxing career Firpo lost a ten round decision to Leonard at the Barre Opera House on November 19, 1931. Mickey Ashline of Plattsburgh, New York, and Mickey Williams of Burlington were also featured in the semi-final bout of six rounds. Ringside seats for the event sold for $2. Young Firpo was managed early on by John J. Comolli, 521 North Main Street, Barre, Vermont.

During a trip to the Teatro Massimo in Italy–L'italo americano Fernando Saldi [Young Firpo] met and became friends with former heavyweight champion of the world, Primo Carnera. Whenever Primo traveled to America, the first thing he would say was–take me to Firpo's restaurant!

After Firpo retired from the rigors of boxing at the urging of his wife Doris, he kept involved with the sport he loved. It wasn't long before he became a fight manager and boxing promoter in the central Vermont area, and brought together many great fighters and great fights to central Vermont fans.

Thursday Night Boxing Cards Big Success–Draws Seven Hundred ***
"Ray Teja Wins by KO in Fifth–Colored Fighters Prove Good Entertainers–Marandola KOs Cyclone Moran In Second Round"

It was like old times again at the armory last night when the boxing fantom of the North Country turned out seven hundred strong to witness the premier of fistic entertainment under the promotion of Young Firpo of Barre who handed the customers a good show. The seven hundred filed out of the National Guard drill hall well pleased after Ray Teja, 154, Barre, Vermont, middleweight champ, floored Battling Downey, 155, Portland, in the fifth round. The supporting card met with wide approval as spectators appeared to take much delight in two colored performers from Portland, namely Johnny Mack who won by a TKO over Frenchy Mars of Barre, and Dark Tiger, 132, who copped a decision over Little Mike Malshuk of Orleans.

In 1948, Firpo got involved with the youth of the area and started a local boxing club. His goals were to bring fighters to enter in the newly established Vermont Golden Gloves in Burlington, and developing champions. His message to these young men, as with so many other trainer/coaches of the time was that if you're going to fight, you need to be in the best of shape. No one stepped into the ring unless they were in top form.

Historical Reflection from The Barre Daily Times, 1948

Local Golden Gloves Candidates Get Drill
"Fight Fans Gather At Auditorium To Watch Boys Work
Under Young Firpo"

Several new Vermont Golden Gloves boxing candidates turned out for the first evening training session, directed by former boxing champ Fernando "Firpo" Saldi at the municipal auditorium gymnasium last evening. A group of fight fans also gathered to watch the ring hopefuls limbering up for future sparring matches and the elimination bouts at the tournament of "pures" in Burlington next month. Among the newcomers to "Young Firpo's" boxing class are Bob Hunt of Montpelier, New England's 185 pound Golden Gloves champ; Dick Comolli, 200 pound Montpelier heavyweight; Harry Perrigo of Barre, UVM freshman and Vermont champion of the 130 pound class; Maurice Kelliher of Roxbury, 168 pounds and winner of his class last year. Others being instructed by Firpo included Paul Laliberte of St. Johnsbury, a Barre art school student who is training for the 135 pound class; Randall Boardman and Donald Saben, both of Northfield, weighting 149 and 143 pounds respectively; the Mattote brothers, Bob and Wendell of Barre, who are in the 126 pound class; Louis Partlow of Northfield, 138 pounds; and Bob "Pop-Eye" Gennette of Barre, training in the 120 pound class.

Firpo's fighters won four championships, with the boxers going on to represent Vermont at the New England Golden Gloves Championships in

Lowell, Massachusetts. These included Wendell Mattotte [featherweight], Henry Bibeau [welterweight], Bob Gale [light heavyweight], and Bob Hunt [heavyweight]–all champions!

In January 1962, Firpo also brought a team to the Vermont Golden Gloves in Burlington that helped develop a future golden gloves champion by the name of Marcel Grimard.

Ferdinand "Firpo" Saldi Passed Away at the Young Age of Seventy-One in 1981

*A Historical Sampling of Early Firpo Bouts ****
Firpo–McGuire a Draw
"Action by Both Last Evening at the Barre Armory"

Young Firpo and Billy McGuire, the two fightingest lightweights to come up the pike in a long time, battled ten grueling rounds to a draw in the main bout of the American Legion boxing card at the armory last evening. The pair was well matched and provided action every bit of the way.

Firpo Takes Decision In Main Bout
"Barre Boy Easily Outpoints Bill Muir of Worcester, Massachusetts: Boxing Fans Get Plenty of Action"

Young Firpo, the top rater among local boxers, took a decision over Billy Muir of Worcester, Massachusetts, in the main bout of a real boxing show presented at the armory last evening by the local post of the American Legion. Fans got action galore in practically every one of the bouts with two knockouts and several knockdowns thrown in for good measure.

Young Firpo Put Out Harvey in 2nd Round
"But It Was A Real Battle As Long As It Lasted: Both Packed Good Punches"

Young Firpo, turning from a back pedaling boxer to a smashing, slugging toe-to-toe fighter, electrified a fight crowd at the Barre Armory last evening when he smashed down Johnny Harvey, bearcat from the Stowe lumber woods, in the second round of the main bout of a card that was crammed with the most intense action from start to finish. There was not a dull second on the card as the boys crashed punches into everything but the customers in the aisle seats.

[October 16, 1932]

Young Firpo Got Decision Over McGuire
"In Grueling 15 Round Battle at Barre Armory Last Night
Some Argument over the Award:
But Young Firpo Seemed to Have Outpointed Lisbon Lumberjack"

Young Firpo, Vermont Welterweight Champion, defeated Billy McGuire, the Lisbon Lumberjack, in a grueling fifteen round battle at the Barre Armory last evening. It was a rough, hard fight, with Firpo, the boxer, piling up a wide margin of points over a more aggressive but rather wild slugger.

[October 25, 1932]

Young Firpo Won Bout From K. O. Kasper
"Though Badly Outweighed, Barre Boy
Furnished a Surprise"

Young Firpo of Barre, proved his title to the Vermont welterweight championship last evening at the Barre Arena when he provided an amazing upset and defeated Johnny K. O. Kasper of Burlington in the ten round main bout of a real action card.

Young Firpo to Meet Renault in Kerns Main Bout

Young Firpo of Barre, Vermont–welterweight champion of this state and the "fightingest" newcomer to show his wares in this city in some time, is returning to town again tonight against Jack Renault by popular demand. The pair met here a couple of weeks ago and after six rounds of the wildest sort of fighting, Renault had shown enough to give him a very slim award.

Young Firpo Beat Gauthier in 5 Rounds
"Referee Colombo Stopped the Bout and Gave It to Barre Man,
Gauthier Had Bandaged Hand and Did Not Use It In
Latter Part of Barre Bout."

Young Firpo, Vermont Welter Champion, won over Al Gauthier of Springfield, Massachusetts, in five rounds last evening in the main bout at the arena. Referee Charles Colombo stopped the bout when it was apparent that Gauthier could not go on.

Young Firpo Took Decision From P. Markey
"Vermont Welterweight Title Holder Carried Every Round:
Had No Trouble in Barre Bout
Burlington Man Didn't Have a Chance Any Time."

Young Firpo, Vermont welterweight title holder, retained his championship easily last evening when he won an eight round decision over Paul Markey of Burlington. Firpo carried every round of the fight.

Young Firpo Evens Up With Jack Renault By
Taking Shade Decision
"Local Welterweight Too Slow in Starting Loses Out
Against Champion of Vermont"

Fistic followers who didn't get their money's worth at last night's boxing bouts in City Hall were either victims of tobacco smoke in their eyes or lacked very much of any type of appreciation. From the opening "wrestling" side-splitter through the main bout in which Young Firpo of Barre, Vermont, evened matters with Jack Renault, the card was packed with action.

[Lewiston Daily Sun]

Young Firpo Easily Wins From Mohawk
"King of Vermont Welterweights Takes No Chances"

Young Firpo, king of the Vermont welters, had little difficulty last evening in subduing wild Kid Mohawk of St. Albans, in the main bout of the boxing show at the armory here last evening, and he took an easy decision over the unpolished visitor in eight rounds.

*** *The Barre Daily Times assorted articles and clippings.*

Barre Opera House lovers gave the historic place a good cleaning in preparation for visitors this week and during Barre's third annual Ethnic Heritage Festival. At left, Alban Richey, vice chairman of the Vermont Center for the Performing Arts, sweeps up. Trustees of the center, along with friends of the Opera House, also uncovered several 1930s posters in good condition, which will be on display during guided tours July 18 from 7 to 10 p.m., and July 19 from 3 to 9 p.m. Below, Fernando Saldi shows off one of those posters — a 1931 model announcing his bout at the Opera House with retired world lightweight champion Benny Leonard.

Reproductions of this poster will be available for sale Friday and Saturday to help raise money to restore and reopen the historic theater.

Article of Fernando Saldi holding boxing poster, Barre Times Argus. Poster found at Barre Opera House.

Young Firpo (right), Bradford, Vermont. Outdoor boxing, 1928.

Ray Teja

Chapter Two

The Beginnings Until 1945
Historical Perspective

How Barre (Vermont) Got It's Name
by Richard Bottamini

The story really begins in 1788 when two pioneers–John Goldsbury and Samuel Rogers and their families decided to quit their places in Massachusetts and trek up into the Green Mountain wilderness, where land was cheap and they could set up new homes. Other pioneers soon followed in short order, coming from Massachusetts, Connecticut, Rhode Island and New Hampshire. They settled in Wildersburgh, nearly 20,000 acres of wild land chartered to William Williams and sixty others in 1780. None of those original chaps ever settled there though, and it took Goldsbury and Rogers to lay the groundwork.

Within a few years, five areas made up Wildersburgh–the Upper Village (now South Barre), the largest of the settlements; the Lower Village (now Barre); Jockey Hollow (the south end of the Lower Village); Gospel Village (now the vicinity around Lincoln School and Elmwood Cemetery); and Thwingville (now North Barre).

As far as the early settlers were concerned, the name Wildersburgh was "for the birds." They wanted something snappier. At the present West Hill Farm in Barre Town, you can find on one of the buildings an attractive sign bearing the inscription–"At a town meeting held at this site September 3, 1793, there occurred a fight between Jonathan Sherman of Barre, Massachusetts, and Captain Thompson of Holden, Massachusetts–for the privilege of naming the town. Sherman won and named the town Barre."

Alack and alas, the town records fail to mention any fight–hence a second legend which is backed up by town records. The townspeople at a meeting in September 1793 decided to erect "a house of worship" and voted that the person "kicking" in the most money for the building would have the right to name the town. Ezekiel Dodge Wheeler came through with £62 (approximately $310), and promptly named the town Barre.

But historian J. W. Ramsay refers to the fight and goes on with this "eye-opening" sentence: "This (the fight) is corroborated by the action of the town which ... twelve years late in September 1805–'voted to destroy the note given by Mr. Wheeler and not collected'–thus carrying the impression that the note was never given a bona fide business transaction."

So, there are two legends–one backed up by town records, and the other coming from the distant past by a tradition (boxing) that just won't go away. Read the evidence and render your own judgment.

A Fight for a Name

Barre Town was organized as Wildersburgh at a town meeting in March 1793 but a few months later, in September of that year, at a special town meeting at the Calvin Smith homestead to raise funds to erect a public meeting house, it was proposed that the man who gave the most toward the building should have the right to re-name the town. Ezekiel Dodge Wheeler bid sixty-two pounds "in lawful money" (then equivalent to $310) and he named the town Barre. But Mr. Wheeler never made good his pledge, he never paid the money. His pledge was later crossed off the town books. This really made the name of Barre invalid. As the story goes, at this same meeting Captain Joseph Thomas of Holden, and Jonathan Sherman from Barre, both in Massachusetts, staged a fist fight. Sherman won, and the name Barre has never been questioned.

Courtesy National Life Ins. Co.

This was on the menu of the Country House Restaurant that was located on Main Street in Barre for many years. (Courtesy of Angela and Robert Brault.)

1929
Allen "Kid" Chaples

"In the Depression years you would fight your sister for some scratch."

Allen Chaples. (Courtesy of Bill Chaples.)

Allen F. Chaples, better known as "Kid" Chaples in his boxing days, was born in Websterville, Vermont, October 13, 1912. He started his boxing career early and had his first match on February 27, 1929, weighing in at a hefty 90 lbs. At the age of sixteen, he won that match–taking a four rounder from a boxer by the name of "Kid" Humphries.

Chaples started his twelve year boxing career very early in life as he loved the competition, and the need for any income he could acquire for his mother and sisters. Along the way, at some point during his many fights, the "Kid" met another family of boxers from Hardwick, Vermont–the Larrabee brothers Vern, Ralph, Max and Earl. It wasn't very long after he met the Larrabee family that he married Ethel, sister of the boxers. Chaples trained with the

Larrabee's and boxed out of Hardwick. Earl Larrabee was the toughest and most powerful boxer of the group, standing at 6'1" tall and weighing in at 215 lbs. Vern became the "Kids" trainer, corner man and best friends. Several tough fighters that Chaples boxed were the Beaupre brothers Charlie and Buster from Burlington, along with a tough blonde middleweight from Newport, Vermont, by the name of Hub Parker. Parker had over 250 fights, but the "Kid" never did get the chance to box him because they weighed in at a different weight class. Chaples only weighed 135 lbs.

The "Kid" used to say, "In times of the depression years, you would fight your sister for some scratch." Often fighting out of shape, and at times not feeling his best, he would hitch a ride, or even walk long distances in all kinds of weather to box for the price of what a pair of boxing shoes cost today!

Chaples remembers many great boxers out of the Barre area including "Dynomite" Dunn from East Barre, who had a string of knock outs, "Midget" Bedell, a fast and clever boxer from Barre who the "Kid" boxed and became friends with to the end. Chaples nephew, Wendell Mattote, was another hard hitting boxer who boxed in the Vermont Golden Gloves in the 1950s. He also boxed Don "KO Frisco" Campbell from Barre several times, as well a friend from Northfield, "Big Yack" Yacavoni.

Allen Chaples eventually moved to Florida and started his own, very successful, masonry business. He had a few fights in Florida, and would come back from time to time to box in his beloved Vermont. The "Kid" idolized World Heavyweight Champion Jack Dempsey, and held in high esteem the great Benny Leonard, and Willie Pep–"The Will of the Wisp"–as he was called.

The "Kid" died from a fall at his Melbourne home at age 82. Allen "Kid" Chaples was a wonderful person who was loved by all–both inside and outside the ring. His record includes 122 fights–69 wins, 30 losses, 20 draws and 3 no decisions.

[Thanks to Allen's son Bill who lives in Northfield, for supplying this infor-mation.]

BOXING

→ This Show Will Help Mayor Burn's

BUSTER
Main
BEAUPR

Burlington, State Welterweight Champion — Always Pleases

SEMI-FINAL 6 ROUNDS

Bobby LaCasse   vs.   Ronnie

Williston
Earns His Promotion Into Semi-final Spot

Burlington — A New
Plenty of Fightir

---

4 ROUND SPECIAL BOUT

K. O. Casper   vs.   Charlie Bea

Burlington

Burlington

Caspar holds a win over Benny Leonard, the former world's champion, and
turns to face Caspar in an exhibition bout.

THIS WILL BE THE FIRST BOXING SHOW UNDER COMMISSION SUPERVISION.
GEORGE WHITNEY, WHITEY KILLICK, W. T. HARRINGTON AND BOB CRONIN,

NOTE! I'LL GUARANTEE THAT BEAUPRE AND MILLER WILL PRODUCE A G
WILL BE ON HAND FOR THIS MAIN E

TICKETS ON SALE: L. P. Wood Sporting Goods Store, Tel. 687
Howard Grill — Tel. 383.   Van Ness Hotel — Tel. 1600
Miss Burlington Diner   Jimmy Rand, Winooski — Tel. 64
George Cioffi at 22 Lake Street in St. Albans — Tel. 36-M

ADM
Reserved 68c
Ringside $1.00
Reserva

emorial Auditorium
LINGTON, VT.   At 8:30 P.M.

RIDAY, AUG. 41 28

for Gifts to Our Boys Joining the Armed Forces ←◄

ut---10 Rounds   **BERNIE**

vs. **MILLER**

Halifax, Nova Scotia — Winner Over Jackie Lifford, Primo
Flores and Anxious To Meet Tommy Jessup

FOUR ROUNDS

on | **Hal Pidgeon** **vs.** **Teddy Dubois**

With
ty | Plattsburg   Shelburne

FOUR ROUNDS

re | **Young Bleau** **vs.** **Mike Vartulli**

South Burlington   Winooski

e re- | Nothing Classy About These Two But They Are Always In There Punching

---

BOXING COMMISSION HEADED BY MAYOR JOHN BURNS, AND ASSISTED BY
NOW HAVE THE FINAL WORD ON ALL BOXING SHOWS IN BURLINGTON.
FIGHT AND EARNESTLY HOPE ALL BOXING FANS, WHO REALLY LIKE FIGHTS,
—BILL LEONARD.

IONS
7c, total 75c
0c, total $1.10
Tel. 383

Judges for this show appointed at Ringside
Referee: Geo. Granai
Matchmaker and Promoter — Bill Leonard
Call Bill Leonard for reservations at Tel. 383

**Soldiers and
Sailors
25c — No Tax**

Where's Buster?
by Bob Winkler

Buster Beaupre, taken December 22, 1941, Y.M.C.A. Gym, Burlington, Vermont.

Buster Beaupre, taken January 8, 1942, Y.M.C.A. Gym, Burlington, Vermont.

Charles "Buster" Beaupre of Burlington, was arguably one of the best Vermont boxers of the first half of the 20th century, but he was just one of the many stellar pugilist of his day. How many of these boxers can you recognize from the past?

Micky "Kid" Williams [Burlington]

Young "Iron Man" Goulette [Burlington]

Jackie Flowers [Syracuse, New York]

"Sailor" Ollie Koski [Bennington]

Sylvester Davis [Worcester, Massachusetts]

"Kid" Jack [Bennington]

Tony Celli [Leominster, Massachusetts]

Tommy Pilk [Oneida, New York]

Ray Teja [East Barre]

"Wildcat" Weeks [Woodsville, New Hampshire]

Bobby Simpson [New Hampshire]

"Young" Ballard [Malletts Bay]

Leo "Graniteville Slugger" Berard

Ernie Jarvis [Burlington]

Art Primrose [Plattsburgh, New York]

Jimmie Grant [Manchester]

Aldo "Kid" Nocchi [Worcester, Massachusetts]

Art "Young" Bissette [Burlington]

Raymond Liberty [Morrisville]

"Kid" Fay [Lakeside, Burlington]

"Kid" Chaples [Hardwick]

"Kid" Burton [Burke]

"Kid" Buster [Johnsonville, New York]

"Young" Caslin [Bennington]

Johnny Adams, [Clinton, Massachusetts]

"Young" Murphy [Worcester, Massachusetts]

"Speed Demon" Kid Cook [Richford/Northfield]

"Young" Silvo [Northfield]

"Young" Conley [North Bennington]

Frankie Costella [Schenectady, New York]

"Kid" Sweeney [Athol, Massachusetts]

Billy Jones [Athol, Massachusetts]

K.O. Montbleau [Canada]

"Kid" Dailey (Joe Sagotta) [North Bennington]

"Young" Winslow [Bennington]

Mike Davies [Burlington]

Charlie Shea [Athol, Massachusetts]

Johnny McCarty [Worcester, Massachusetts]

"Wild" Freddie Wright [Bennington]

"Young" Flynn [Stamford]

Al Parker [Athol, Massachusetts]

Harvey Pierce [Clinton/Orange, Massachusetts]

Jackie "the Beebe Bomber" Fournier [Lakeside, Burlington]

Bob Mercier [Waterbury, CCC]

Perle Gates [Bennington]

Harold Gokey [St. Albans]

Charlie "Buster" Beaupre [Burlington]

"Kid" O'Brien [Burlington]

Johnny House [Winooski]

Billy Robinson [Burlington]

"Kid" Jack [Bennington]

Mike Fusco [Albany, New York]

K.O. Kasper "Fighting Blacksmith" [Burlington]

"Irish" Paddy Flynn [Boston]

Larry Mercier [Hardwick]

Francis Marino [Bennington]

Lou Bogchetti [North Adams, Massachusetts]

Gerald Markey [Burlington]

Fritzie (Frankie) "Young" Weiss [Albany, New York]

Bob Michaud [Hardwick]

Willie Gibson [Albany, New York]

"Young" Moquin [Burlington]

"Young" Paulus [Lakeside, Burlington]

"Kid Morgan" [St. Albans]

"Kid" Stewart [Plainfield]

Abe Nathan [Burlington; Portland, Maine]

Chick Suggs [St. Albans]

"Cowboy" Hugh Patterson [Charlotte]

"Roughhouse" Rogers [Burlington]

King Phillips [St. Albans]

Tommy Murphy [Albany, New York]

"Battling" Pinney [Chester]

Angelo Manna [Worchester, Massachusetts]

"Kid" Herman [Leominister, Massachusetts]

Jack Reno [Rickers Mills CCC, Groton State Forest]

Bobby Simpson [Tilton, New Hampshire]

"Young" Surdam [Bennington]

Frank Augustini [Albany, New York]

"Young" McCoy [Worchester, Massachusetts]

"Young" Trombley [Charlotte]

Mickey Walker [Bennington Flats]

Joe Peleuso [Albany, New York]

Bill Mackey [Worchester, Massachusetts]

"Young" Hogan [Orange, Massachusetts]

Eppie Stearns [Orange, Massachusetts]

Albert Zelespe [Hoosick Falls, New York]

"Young" Flanagan [Athol, Massachusetts]

"Battling" Yac [Northfield]

Mike Moran [Lowell, Massachusetts/US Navy]

Kenneth "Kid" Bushway [Burlington]

Young Cohen [Burlington]

"Cyclone" Moran [Barre]

Young Ladue [South Burlington]

Walt "Slugger" Neal [Barre]

Elvear Rioux [Quebec]

Whitey Allen (Hebert Allard) [Berlin, New Hampshire]

"Cannon Ball" Cote [Lewiston, Maine]

"Kid" Economu [Fairfax]

"Kid" Fortin [St. Albans]

Jimmy Riley [Montreal]

Irish Tim Bitts [Three Rivers, Quebec]

Sailor White [Burlington]

Danny "Baby Face" O'Connell [Montreal]

Mickey Ashline [Plattsburgh, New York]

Jerry Bernard [Troy, New York]

Johnny Morris [Montreal]

K.O. Laughlin [Ft. Ethan Allen, Colchester]

Kid Coiffi [St. Albans]

Young Tracy [Montreal]

Ken Petrie [Fairfield]

Battling Fitz [St. Albans]

Young Jerry [Essex Junction]

Pat Ward [Fairfax]

Slugger Putvah [St. Albans]

Mickey Williams [Burlington]

Ernie Jarvis [Essex Junction]

Sid Cook [Plattsburgh, New York]

Red Benson [Plattsburgh, New York]

Gunner Brown [Burlington]

Young Lefty [Rutland]

Harry Scott [Holyoke, Massachusetts]

Clyde Markey [Burlington]

Young Gardner [West Albany]

Tom Grady [Springfield]

Tommy Phillips [Worchester, Massachusetts]

"Flash" Gamble [Savannah, Georgia]

"Kid" Buster [Johnsonville, New York]

Art Chapdelaine [Springfield]

Carlo Duponde [Springfield]

Bam Guyette [Manchester]

K.O. Jones [Syracuse, New York]

Roger Fournier [Websterville]

"Kid" Baker [Camp Wildwood, Woodsville, New Hamphire]

Sid Jarvis [East Barre]

Ray Audette [Graniteville]

"Kid" Campo [Graniteville]

Al Schmelling [East Barre]

Jack Perry (Dan Pericone) [Wells River]

Billy Mitchell (Artie Irwin) [Rickers Mills]

Jack Maloney [Barre]

"Kid" Shadow [East Barre]

Jimmy Marsha [Barre]

"Dynamite" Dunn [Barre Town]

Max Baer [Barre Town]

"Kid" Kaplin [Barre]

* * * * * * *

Some Early Vermont Boxing Venues

Burlington Memorial Auditorium [New 1928]

VFW Hawks [Union Street] Auditorium, Bennington

Aldrich Hall, Graniteville

Granite Street Hall, Barre

Champlain Valley Exposition

Northfield Armory

Meadow Brook Arena, North Adams, Massachusetts

Woodman Hall, Burlington

Camp Wildwood, New Hampshire

Milton Grange Hall

Bennington Armory

Concurrent Military Training Camp, Winooski

Lamoille Valley Fair

Rickers Mills CCC [Civilian Conservation Corp]

Waterbury CCC

The Class of 43
("Open Letter to Buster")
by Bob Winkler

Dear Buster,

I hope you don't mind me calling you Buster. It's just that I remember my father and uncles talking about you around the dinner table, and there always seemed to be a ring of excitement going on when your name came up. The lady folk would go off into the parlor when boxing talk took up. There was always alot of what ifs and it should have been thrown into the conversation. So, I'm wondering whether you knew that hometown people everywhere were talking about you, and whether they bothered you when they saw you on the street, or tried to talk to you after a fight.

It seems as though you've been around a long time, but I know that if you started to fight when you were nineteen, say, that perhaps our ages aren't that far apart, that perhaps you might consider me a friend, and have a drink with me and my buddies one day when I return from the front.

My mother never approved of me sneaking out of my house at night with my friend, Nick, to see you at the Memorial Hall. The excitement was just too great not to take that chance of being caught and getting a beating for my efforts when I tried to sneak back into the house late at night. I owe a lot to you for my boyhood dreams, and just wanted to thank you for that.

But, I'm also wondering while I sit here crouched in my foxhole whether you remember your family, or how close you are to them. Do the dreams of glory still ring true, or does the lure of money make you do things that might not be considered always right?

I think I want to go to college when I get out of the service. I know that's probably not going to happen, but I'd like to be a teacher. I see a lot of kids over here misplaced by the war and I'm thinking I might want to work with them, maybe get them into a gym to box. What do you think? I know that probably won't happen, but I'd like it to.

I'm scared Buster. I'm not even sure that I'll make it back to the States. My family worries terribly. If I sent you a letter, could you deliver it to them? That'd mean a lot to me. I miss Burlington and paling around with my friends. My friend, Joe, in the 2nd Battalion was killed the other day. He lived just down the street from me and we used to walk to school together, and get into lots of trouble, of course.

I apologize for bothering you, Buster, and I know you have other things to worry about right now. I'm hoping you win that bout in New York against Bummy Davis that I read about in the Stars & Stripes. How do you feel before a big fight? Most likely how I feel now. It's terribly cold here, and lonely–and we're expecting a major attack tomorrow.

So, I'm wondering what future generations might think about members of their family boxing while a war is going on. Maybe it helps to get ready. Well, I expect that somebody will want to know about their past, a daughter, or grandchild perhaps, and they'll dig around in old newspapers trying to find a trace of that past. Some people will remember, but won't want to talk. Others will give up musty paper clippings with no dates that will merely give whispers back to the good old days.

Still, they were good, weren't they? I mean, I only hope that what we're sacrificing for over here has been done with dignity. I think I miss those old days already. I know I miss my family terribly.

Evans Elzear Way
European Theater, January 4, 1944

—————————————————————

This imaged letter captures the romance of small town boxing in the World War II era of Vermont. It is not a real letter but was constructed as a result of a lot of related material of letters and old records that were gathered for this book.

Even though it is not real, it is real in the minds of people interested in history and the sweet science of boxing. This letter captures the spirit of this book.

Nelson Brice, Trainer

Introducing a sports legend isn't easy, and legends are made not born. Such is the case with Charlie Buster Beaupre. Indeed, all of the research indicates that it wasn't always an easy road that Buster traveled, but for more than a decade he was Vermont's brightest shining star, amongst a galaxy of aspiring pugilist. There is much yet to be done in uncovering the sport of boxing in Vermont, which offers a rich and colorful class of participants. It is only hoped here that the door has been opened a crack, and that future family genealogist will continue to search for the truth, and in the process learn more about themselves.

One final note before we pick up the journey with Buster. The following appeared in the Sports-I-Vents column written by Wendell LaLime of the Newport Daily Express, May 5, 1943.

Boxing comes to light right here in Vermont through the efforts of our old friend, Nelson [Longfellow*] Brice, over in Burlington. Brice, who has managed several prominent Vermont boxers, including Buster Beaupre, and who has supplied boxing shows in Newport with some outstanding talent in the past, appears now to be taking advantage of a lull in the game and devoting his time toward building for the future. Brice has an entire stable of youngsters working out of the Y.M.C.A. gym over there, and the manner in which these kids go at it is really something to behold.

The program that Brice has prescribed for the Burlington students of the manly art calls for a rigorous workout that includes everything in the book–fast bag, heavy bag, jump rope, shadow boxing, routine exercise and actual boxing–nothing sissy about the routine at all.

Scribe Whitey Killick writes that while there seems to be little possibility of these kids getting any action for some time, and most of them are too young for the pro game, they are getting a good deal of benefit out of the work. If they never hit a lick in the ring, at least they are going to be able to take care of themselves in a personal emergency, and personal emergencies have a way of confronting youngsters these days.

Perhaps we can see the beginnings of the Vermont Golden Gloves in the rigorous workouts displayed by Mr. Brice's young pugilist the Y.M.C.A.

Bob Wrinkler, Burlington, Vermont, January 5, 2008
*Attributed to Gil Wood–Sportraits

Nelson A. Brice, Sr., 56, of 39 King Street, in Burlington, died on September 28, 1970. He was born in Burlington on May 28, 1914, son of the late Anthony and Fida (Raymond) Brice. From 1948 to 1959 he was proprietor of the Brice Caf. He then became self-employed in the taxi business as an independent driver with the City Cab Company of Burlington. He had also been an active supporter of Boys Town and many other youth projects in the Burlington area. In the 1930s, he actively managed many amateur and professional boxers in New England.

The Burlington Free Press, September 29, 1970, p. 10

RKO Sports Spotlight: A Popular Vermont Pugilist Weighs In
Charlie "Buster" Beaupre

Bennington Armory–Young Beaupre, 135, TKO over
Harry Scott, Holyoke, Massachusetts (4)
Bennington Evening Banner, October 6, 1933, p. 6

Plattsburg, New York–Buster Beaupre, Burlington, KO'd Art Primrose
Plattsburg: June 1934

Bennington, Vermont–Buster Beaupre, Burlington, win over
Jimmie Grant, Manchester (4)
*July 1934: Bennington Union Street Auditorium bouts
sponsored by VFW Post 1332*

Bennington, Vermont–Charlie "Young" Beaupre, 135, Burlington,
Vermont Lightweight Champion, TKO over
Tommy Phillips, 135, Worcester, Massachusetts (6)
Bennington Evening Banner, November 2, 1934, p. 6

Bennington, Vermont–Charlie "Buster" Beaupre, Burlington, Vermont
Lightweight Champion, Decision over
Aldo "Kid" Nocchi, Worcester, Massachusetts (6)
Bennington Evening Banner, November 9, 1934, p. 6

Fort Ethan Allen–Buster Beaupre, Burlington, TKO over
Timinski, Fort Ethan Allen (3)
Boxing Program, May 27, 1938

Fort Ethan Allen–Buster Beaupre, Burlington vs Forkas, Fort Ethan Allen
Boxing Tournament, Third smoker/First Program, December 29, 1938

Fort Ethan Allen–Buster Beaupre, Burlington, Decision over
Liberacki, Fort Ethan Allen (6)
*Boxing Tournament–Third smoker/Fourth Program, March 17, 1939
*Buster hurt his right hand in the second round when he floored Liberacki in
that round. In (the) sixth Buster was hurt at (the) end of the round in the ribs.*

Burlington, Vermont–Buster Beaupre, 139 1/2, Burlington,
KO'd Jackie Taylor, 140, Brooklyn (4)
Fitchburg [Massachusetts] Sentinel, August 22, 1941, p. 8

Burlington, Vermont–Buster Beaupre, 139 1/2, Burlington, beat
Al Dunbar, 140, New York (1)
Reno Evening Gazette, November 15, 1941, p. 11

Burlington, Vermont–Buster Beaupre, 140 1/2, Burlington, has stopped
Eddie Buerra, 146 3/4, New York (6)
Reno Evening Gazette, December 5, 1941, p. 22

Burlington, Vermont–Frankie Conti, 135 1/2, Haverhill, Massachusetts,
out-pointed Buster Beaupre, 139, Vermont (10)
Reno Evening Gazette, January 30, 1942, p. 18

Burlington, Vermont–Frankie Conti, 135 1/2, Haverhill, Massachusetts,
out-pointed Buster Beaupre, 139, Vermont (10)
Lowell Sun & Citizen Leader, January 30, 1942, p. 19

Burlington, Vermont–Buster Beaupre, 139, Burlington, and
Frankie Conti, 136, Haverhill, Draw (10)
Fitchburg (Massachusetts) Sentinel, February 27, 1942, p. 8

Burlington, Vermont–Gene Johnson, 145, New York, stopped
Buster Beaupre, 146, Burlington (8)
Reno Evening Gazette, March 20, 1942, p. 16

Burlington, Vermont–Buster Beaupre, 140, Burlington, out pointed
Gene Johnson, 139 1/2, Montreal (10)
Reno Evening Gazette, April 11, 1942, p. 11

Burlington, Vermont–Buster Beaupre, 139, Burlington, out-pointed
Ernie Cooper, 135, Jersey City, New Jersey (10)
Lowell Sun & Citizen Leader, May 16, 1942, p. 6

Burlington, Vermont–Buster Beaupre, 139, Burlington, out-pointed
Frankie Conti, 137, Haverhill, Massachusetts (10)
Reno Evening Gazette, June 27, 1942, p. 9

Burlington, Vermont–Bernie Miller, 139, New York, won by TKO over
Buster Beaupre, 140, Burlington (4)
Fitchburg Sentinel, August 29, 1942, p. 5

Boston–Two up and coming welterweights will stage the eight round semi-final at the arena, Dave "Golden Boy" Andrews of Lowe (1), Massachusetts and Buster Beaupre of Burlington, Vermont
Fitchburg [Massachusetts] Sentinel, January 8, 1943, p. 8

Boston–Matchmaker Eddie Mack has lined up six supporting bouts, headed by an eight round semi-final, which pits Buster Beaupre of Burlington, Vermont, against Frankie MacDougal of Boston.
Berkshire Evening Eagle [Pittsfield, Massachusetts], February 11, 1943, p. 14

Boston–Jumping from boxing ridiculous to the sublime, we have been tipped that the next hurdle that will be set up on Sammy Fuller's comeback track will be the fistic pride of Burlington, Vermont, one Buster Beaupre, at Mechanics a week from tonight ... Buster is reputed to be a very ambitious fisticuffer ... But he'll have to be a very smart one to get anywhere with smart Sammy, who has forgotten more than most of the current crop of battlers have had an opportunity to learn.
Berkshire Evening Eagle [Pittsfield], February 25, 1943, p. 14

Fall River, Massachusetts–Al Evans, 147, Newport, Rhode Island, stopped Buster Beaupre, 144, Burlington, Vermont (7)
Reno Evening Gazette, April 30, 1943, p. 14

New Haven, Connecticut–Julie Kogan, 134 1/2, New Haven, KO'd Buster Beaupre, 140, Burlington, Vermont (7)
Reno Evening Gazette, December 28, 1943, p. 12

New York–Al "Bummy" Davis, 147, New York, KO'd [98 seconds] Buster Beaupre, 143, Burlington, Vermont (1)
*Reno Evening Gazette, January 19, 1944, p. 12
& March 17, 1944, p. 16*

Bennington, Vermont–Buster Beaupre of Burlington, and Jackie Flowers of Worcester will meet in the main boxing bout at Bennington tomorrow night. The semi-final will bring together George Frederico of Schenectady and Johnny Abbott of Worcester. Arthur E. Lemieux of 209 Beech Street, Bennington, promotes the bouts in that city and would like to hear from any manager in Berkshire who has a capable boxer.
Berkshire Evening Eagle [Pittsfield], February 21, 1946, p. 4

Burlington, Vermont–Buster Beaupre, 141, Burlington, KO'd
Phil Beltram, 140, Montreal (1)
The Berkshire County Eagle, February 27, 1946, p. 12

Rutland, Vermont–Buster Beaupre, 141, Burlington, out-pointed
Jackie Brynn, 145, Toronto (8)
Berkshire Evening Eagle [Pittsfield], March 8, 1946, p. 12

Barre, Vermont–Buster Beaupre, 140, Burlington, TKO
John LaRue, 144, Brockton, Massachusetts (8)
Berkshire Evening Eagle [Pittsfield], April 12, 1946, p. 18

Burlington, Vermont–Buster Beaupre, 139, Burlington, stopped
Joe Coughlin, 146, Toronto, (6)
Berkshire County Eagle, April 17, 1946, p. 19

Bangor, Maine–Ralph Walton, 142, Montreal, KO'd
Buster Beaupre, 146, Burlington, Vermont (4)
Fitchburg [Massachusetts] Sentinel, May 9, 1946

Lewiston, Maine–Lefty Lachance, 140, Lisbon, KO'd
Buster Beaupre, 144 1/2, Burlington (4)
Berkshire Evening Eagle [Pittsfield], December 3, 1946, p. 14

Burlington, Vermont–Buster Beaupre, 143, Burlington, out-pointed
Ruby Margolin, 149, Montreal (10)
Fitchburg (Massachusetts) Sentinel, December 11, 1946, p. 8

Burlington, Vermont–Buster Beaupre, 141, Burlington, out-pointed
Maurice "Lefty" Lachance, 143, Lewiston, Maine (10)
Berkshire Evening Eagle [Pittsfield], December 20, 1946, p. 24

Barre, Vermont–Buster Beaupre, 143, Burlington, and
Billy Napper, 141, Boston, Draw (10)
Fitchburg [Massachusetts] Sentinel, January 31, 1947, p. 8

Burlington, Vermont–Dave Castilloux, 138, Montreal, KO'd
Buster Beaupre, 142, Burlington (7)
Fitchburg [Massachusetts] Sentinel, March 21, 1947, p. 8

Burlington, Vermont–Buster Beaupre, 141, Burlington, KO'd
Al Michaud, 143 1/2, Sanford, Maine (4)
Berkshire Evening Eagle [Pittsfield], April 17, 1947, p. 24

Chapter Three

Golden Days Since 1946
Memories Within Our Times

Henry Bibeau
"You're a lamp, one blow and you're out!"

From Left to Right: "Popeye" Bob Gennette; Wendell Mattote; Firpo Saldi; Bob Hunt, Heavyweight; Henry Bibeau, Welterweight.

Henry was born in 1930, growing up in Lower Graniteville, Vermont, and at the age of ten showed an interest in boxing. The year was 1940 when his dad built a boxing ring in their barn for him and his brothers, and their neighbors Marcel and Rene Grimard. Through their teen years, the Bibeau's and Grimard's boxed each other many times. It wasn't long before the word spread that the Bibeau family had a gym, and many guys would stop by on the weekends to step into the ring to see who could "lick" who. Henry was in charge of the gym as a trainer and boxer. "There were many battles, black eyes, and bleeding noses. Many weekends of good clean fun which kept us in shape and busy," Henry remembered.

Young Bibeau started boxing competitively at the age of fourteen. By 1949, at age eighteen, Henry got serious about the sport of boxing and started training under the watchful eye of Firpo Saldi, whom he called the "best trainer ever." Saldi trained his boxers in the basement of the Barre Auditorium. There was quite a group of boxers including "Popeye" Gennette, Wendell Mattote, Bob Hunt, Bob Gale and Ken Ball, to name a few.

Henry entered the Vermont Golden Gloves that year as a 147 lb open class boxer. He boxed his way into the finals defeating Bernard Yandow of Burlington for the championship. The next stop for the Vermont champion was the New England Golden Gloves Tournament of Champions in Lowell, Massachusetts. There Henry faced a real tough boxer for the New England Title by the name of Norman Hayes of Boston. Hayes beat Bibeau in a tough fight, and later turned pro as a middleweight and fought Jake "Bronx Bull" LaMotta twice–beating LaMotta at Boston Garden in January 1952 on a split decision, then losing to the "Bronx Bull" by unanimous decision at Olympia Stadium in Detroit in March the same year.

The loss for the New England title was not the end of the road for Henry as he continued boxing through the 1950s and early 60s, compiling a very impressive record of 52 wins and 10 losses. He continued boxing in the Vermont Golden Gloves tournaments as well as various "smokers"–or club bouts–throughout the state. Henry moved up in weight through the years from 147 lbs to heavyweight. While stationed with the Marine Corps at Camp Pendleton, California in 1953, Henry boxed in various events in the 160 and 175 lb classes.

Henry worked the night shift with the Barre City Police Department for over 30 years. His fellow police officers would chide Henry telling him "you're nothing but a lamp (or perhaps candle)–one blow and you're out!" It was during the 1962 Vermont Golden Gloves Tournament in Burlington Memorial Auditorium that the lamp went out. While making a comeback in the heavyweight division, Henry faced an older, but powerful, boxer in Andy Anderson of Whitehall, New York. It was in the third round when Anderson connected, knocking Henry out and in the process breaking his jaw when he hit the canvas. Anderson went on to win the Vermont Golden Gloves Championship that year. Henry proved his fellow officers wrong–as the lamp stayed lit for many years for the boxing police officer.

After 1962, Henry went on to train boxers in the Barre Boxing Club. He trained, amongst others, Mike Poulin of Brookfield, who participated in the Vermont Golden Gloves as well as club bouts throughout the state.

With an amateur career of 62 bouts Henry faced many opponents including Bernard Yandow, Andy Anderson, Burton Burnette and Forrest Rouelle who went to St. Michael's College and then on to becoming a Catholic Priest.

Henry P. Bibeau, in his 70s, is retired and resides in Williamstown, Vermont. Henry is quoted as saying, "I never got married but always had a "babe", and still do." Maybe that lamp is still lit!

Andy Anderson is standing over Henry Bibeau, January 25, 1962. (Courtesy of Narcis Goselyn.)

Like Father Like Son: Plattsburgh's Boxing Frankie and Wendell "Buddy" DeCarlo

Frank DeCarlo started his boxing career as a teenager in Philadelphia where he grew up. Though he never boxed in the Golden Gloves, he saw plenty of action. His travels eventually led him to Plattsburgh where he was remembered by local boxing fans as a member of the 26th Infantry boxing and wrestling team. By April 1946, he was hitting the comeback trail boxing at the LaSalle gymnasium in Troy, New York, and heading the movement at the local Veterans of Foreign Wars post to interest young men in boxing. His efforts paid off and he trained numerous boxers in the Plattsburgh area including his son, Buddy, who went on to win many Vermont Golden Glove titles. Frank always had a very tough and well trained team ready for the gloves through the 1950s and early 1960s. His training headquarters was an old firehouse called the Horicon Engine and Hose Company, No. 3.

Horicon Engine and Hose Company, No. 3.

Horicon Engine and Hose Co. No. 3 Museum.

Frank boxed in the military in 1934 while in the service in Plattsburgh, and also in Hawaii where he made a name for himself. He was called "Deadpan" DeCarlo because of his lack of expression, so his opponents could never tell whether he was hurt. Around Plattsburgh he was one of the best, not only in the ring, but with his expertise at training youngsters. After he retired from boxing with over 112 fights to his credit, he went into the plumbing and heating business. Frank passed away in 1969.

Wendell "Buddy" DeCarlo started boxing when he was sixteen, and entered the Vermont Golden Gloves for the first time in 1959–in the 147 pound open division. He boxed many years in the gloves, eventually progressing to the 160 pound class. Of course, his father Frankie trained him. Buddy didn't mind sparring, but hated running to build up his wind. "I would run every night but I hated it," Buddy recalled. He trained at the Plattsburgh Boys Club and at the Air Force base, where he sparred with anybody and everybody, no matter what they weighed. If there were no sparring partners, his father would get into the ring with him, and... "sparring with my dad would really toughen me up," said the younger DeCarlo.

Buddy won the Vermont Golden Gloves [1960-62] and went on to the New England Gloves Tournament of Champions in Lowell, Massachusetts, which he won, advancing to the New York City Golden Gloves that year.

Some of the toughest opponents Buddy stepped into the ring with included: W. Payne, Wilber "Skeeter" McClure, Johnny Folks, Ed Owens and John Cokley–who had over 200 amateur fights to his credit. Buddy boxed him three times–winning one, losing one, and one ending in a draw. Buddy also won the AAU championship in Albany, New York, and went on to the nationals in Toledo, Ohio. In 1960, he lost a match against "Skeeter" McClure who went on to win the gold medal in the 156 pound class in the 1960 Olympics. ["Skeeter's" roommate at the Olympics was none other than Cassius Clay, who also won the "gold" in the 175 pound class]. When asked what kind of fighter "Skeeter" was, Buddy remarked–"He was the full package"–in other words he was the best. Buddy traveled throughout the United States boxing in Golden Gloves and AAU [the forerunner to USA Boxing] national tournaments.

Buddy remembers promoter/manager-trainer Ben Becker out of the Albany, New York area, once saying that Carmen Basilio would never amount to anything in boxing. "He was certainly wrong on that one," recalled Buddy. Basilio–"The Onion Farmer" from Canastota, New York, won world championships as a welterweight and middleweight. The International Hall of

Plattsburgh Boys' Club

Famer ended his boxing career in 1961 with a record of 56 wins [27 knockouts], 16 losses, and 7 draws.

Buddy says that his biggest regret was not attending Carmen's training camp to train with heavyweight Mike DeJean. He always liked boxing in Lowell and after only nine fights he had the opportunity to box in Boston Gardens in a national tournament. Buddy always had a good time boxing. "I knocked out many of my opponents," Buddy recalled.

Buddy's boxing career came to an end after he married in 1962. He started a new life becoming a welder and fitter–retiring from the trade after 47 years. Along the way he joined the military and served a tour in Vietnam in 1967. With a record of 50 wins [19 KO's] and only 12 losses, Buddy DeCarlo was the "full package" himself, and arguably one of the best boxers to come out of the Northern Country.

1948
Bernard "Bernie" Cummings, Sr.

Bernie Cummings, Sr.

Bernie Cummings was involved in Vermont Golden Gloves for fifty years, beginning in 1942. He fought in the Navy, and professionally appeared in bouts in the Boston Garden and the Buffalo Civic Center, where he fought a grueling battle with the #10 ranked contender in the world. In 1948, Bernie managed one of Vermont's most successful boxing teams in the first Golden Gloves Tournament, and he would continue to do so throughout the 1950s. Later on he took over as Tournament Director for the Vermont Sunday News. In the early 1970s he was asked by Governor Thomas Salmon to take over as Commissioner of Boxing for the state of Vermont, and served in that position for more than 30 years.

As commissioner he took a lot of punches, and dealt a few blows–but his #1 concern was always for the safety and welfare of the fighters and the amateur boxing program in the state of Vermont. It was during this time that Bernie was able to meet and shake the hand of three time world heavyweight champion, Muhammad Ali.

Before he was appointed Boxing Commissioner, Bernie served as the Director of the Burlington Boys' Club, where his fundraising events, like the Outdoor Recreation show, were held annually at Memorial Auditorium. Few knew about Bernie's boxing career or his other athletic abilities until the time he was appointed Chairman of the Vermont Boxing Commission around 1974. Shortly after his appointment, Bernie along with Ernie Dague–who was eventually appointed to the commission–showed up at the Enosburg Opera House where Jim Sheridan and Ernie Farrar put on regularly scheduled club shows or "smokers." They were both greatly surprised that a member of the boxing commission would take part or show any interest in the local events that were taking place. It just so happened that another referee was needed that evening, and Bernie immediately volunteered. It was hard to believe that the chair of the Vermont Boxing Control Board was in the ring refereeing bouts!

Bernie the "Comish"

There were problems within the boxing circles in Vermont in the early 1970s, and Bernie's appointment as Chairman of the Vermont Boxing Control Board came as the result of a fact finding commission hearing in Montpelier in April 1974. The hearing had been requested by parties interested in upgrading the Boxing Control Boards position, and improving the direction of boxing throughout the state. Bernie was asked to attend the hearing–as he had been a professional boxer himself as well as a trainer, manager, coach and promoter of amateur boxing through the years–but more so as Executive Director of the Burlington Boys' Club and his work with area youth for some twenty-five years.

Bernie had been asked by a commission member if he would accept an appointment to the board. At the time the control board or commission was getting some bad press, and Bernie said absolutely not, he didn't need that in his life. The fact finders though wanted input from Bernie, and input they got! Bernie went to the hearing prepared with ideas on how to improve the workings of the control board, and the direction of boxing in the state. Finally, after some further coaxing Bernie agreed to submit his name–while waiting to see what happened.

Representative Andrew Sullivan monitored the hearing, and it was his recommendation that Cummings get the appointment. Bernie replaced Reuben Levin of Bennington whose term on the board had expired. Jim Fitzgerald of St. Albans, was also appointed to the board replacing David Carr of Burlington who officially announced his resignation at the Montpelier hearing. Dr. Nolan Cain, a Burlington physician, retained his position on the board.

When Bernie took over as chair of the Vermont Boxing Control Board there were many coaches, trainers and promoters that would put on shows with little regard for the rules of the game. Bernie immediate sought to make necessary changes for the betterment of the sport in Vermont. Commission members began attending every boxing event in the state. Bernie was going to make sure that the boxing rules, though severely outdated, would be followed.

Never one to see a boxer get hurt in the ring, Bernie would sit at ringside keeping a close eye on the boxers. If the match appeared one-sided or out of hand, he would signal the ref to stop the bout. That's the way Bernie was–safety of the boxer was first and foremost. Years before the start of the Vermont Golden Gloves Tournament, Bernie suggested that more padding was needed in the ring, so if a boxer fell they wouldn't suffer an injury. There was some disagreement on the matter–but Bernie prevailed and ordered gym padding on top of an inch thick pad to be placed on the canvas. Boxers began complaining that they couldn't move their feet very well, were getting very tired, and ended up twisting their ankles. The extra padding finally came to an end after one boxer ended up breaking his ankle.

Rejuvenation of the Gloves

In October 1976, George McGuane of the Lowell [Massachusetts] Sun was looking for a new tournament director for the Vermont Golden Gloves. The "gloves" had been dormant in Vermont for about three years, and The Lowell Sun, as franchise holder of Golden Gloves in New England–and George as its director–wanted Vermont back in the fray once again. The Green Mountain State had been involved with Lowell and the golden gloves since the mid-forties. Bernie had taken several Vermont championship teams to the New England Golden Gloves Tournament of Champions in Lowell through the years, so he and George had become good friends. Bernie suggested Ernie Farrar, a broadcaster with WVMT radio. Ernie had little experience with tournaments, except though promoting local club shows with Jimmy Sheridan at the Franklin County Boxing Club. The other problem was that George wanted to rejuvenate the Vermont Golden Gloves tournament in January 1977–just a few months away! Who better to call than Bernie Cummings. The next day Bernie and several community supporters of the gloves met with Ernie and offered their help. Needless to say George McGuane was very grateful that Vermont was coming back into the fold.

The Burlington Boys' Club gym was used the first year for practice as well as the tournament–with the capacity of two hundred. With the help of Burt Riley and Bob Lombard of the Village Sports Shop in Milton, the club was able to secure much needed equipment. The next year the gloves were held at Winooski High School, and the following year went back to Burlington Memorial Auditorium where it had started in the mid-1940s.

Bernie–The Early Years

Bernie was one of the best athletes to ever come out of Burlington High School. A standout football and baseball player, he was co-captain of the football team and was a running back, and in baseball he roamed the outfield. He was recruited by the Brooklyn Dodgers, and signed a contract with their minor league club out of Oleans, New York. His baseball career was cut short though, when he was released from the club to join the service.

Bernie never boxed in the amateur ranks, but fought professionally at the age of fifteen when he was still in high school. He was a boxer-puncher middleweight noted for his courage. He served a tour in the U. S. Navy where he received a World War II Medal of Victory. Bernie also boxed while in the Navy. Bernie did his boxing in the 1940s era of Tony Zale and Rocky Graziano–who are among the all-time great middleweights. Bernie fought out of Boston, New York, Montreal, Syracuse and other Northeast cities.

Bernie studied Boys' Club work at New York University and Springfield College, and became Director of the Burlington Boys' Club in 1949–a position he held for forty years–retiring in 1989. Through the years he was a guidance counselor, youth leader and teacher to thousands of boys in the Burlington area. Bernie had a lasting influence on the boys he came in contact with at the Burlington Boys' Club [now the Burlington Boys' and Girls' Club]. In later years, they would proudly recall their association with him, and refer to themselves as Boys' Club alumni. He counseled growing boys who often times would go astray were it not for his advice and interest in their welfare. Bernie received many awards through the years for caring for youth and getting them on the right track in life. Bernie also started several "Silver Mittens" programs around the area–a program whereby youngsters could get involved with boxing.

Bernie Cummings (left) and Muhammad Ali (right).

The End of an Era

The boxing community was saddened with the passing of Bernard Robert Cummings, Sr., at the age of seventy-five, on June 19, 2002. He and his wife, Anita, made their home in Winooski, and Bernie will be remembered as a loving husband, father, grandfather, brother, uncle, friend and mentor.

Bernie did a lot for the good of boxing in the state of Vermont. He was an excellent commissioner, and always looked out for the welfare and safety of all boxers involved in the sport. Every year when the bell rings to start the first bout of the Vermont Golden Gloves tournament, Bernie will be remembered for helping to bring back the Golden Gloves on track in 1977. Thanks Bernie–rest in peace.

Wendell Mattote / Rocky Mattote

"When the bell rang you knew you were in for a tough evening."

Wendell Mattote (left), Frenchy Demars (center), "Popeye" Gennett (right).

Mattote and Mattote were father and son boxers out of Barre, Vermont, and a couple of tough hombres. Wendell Mattote started boxing when he was eighteen, and had one of the best and well known trainers in the state, Firpo Saldi, who trained his boxing team in the basement of the Barre Auditorium. Wendell was the toughest and best of his 126 lb weight class winning the 1949 Vermont Golden Gloves Championship by defeating Joe Lacharite of Winooski. Both were very clever boxers, but Mattote landed the blows, and was more effective in the clinches. In the final round, Wendell wore down Lacharite and gained an unanimous decision. When asked how tough Wendell was, Allen Shangraw–many times Vermont Golden Gloves 126 lb

Wendell Mattote

Rocky Mattote, right, vs Charlie Joyal, left. 1983 VTGG 175 lb. Championship.

champion—he replied, "Wendell Mattote was the toughest boxer I ever faced in the ring. He was well trained and in the best of shape, and when the bell rang you knew you were in for a tough evening." Wendell also won the 1950 126 lb Championship.

Wendell boxed some tough customers throughout the state including his hometown at the Union Hall, the Barre Armory (currently the Elks Club), Northfield and Burlington.

Wendell's son, Mike "Rocky" Mattote, also started boxing in 1977. Mike was out of the same boxing mold as his father—very tough and knew how to box! Mike was in the finals of the 1979 Vermont Golden Gloves and won the championship in 1982 at 160 lbs, and was the Vermont Golden Gloves champion in 1983 at 175 pounds. He boxed throughout Vermont, Massachusetts, Maine and Canada, compiling a very impressive record of 38 wins and 12 losses. Mike "Rocky" Mattote was one tough seasoned boxer.

1951
Ronnie Begins
Burlington Boys' Club "Surprise Package"
by Kim Pulley

Ronnie Begins

Ronnie Begins was a Vermont Golden Gloves Champion well known throughout the state, and a celebrity of sorts in local Sports circles. Newspapers like the Burlington Free Press, the Lowell [Massachusetts] Sun and the Plattsburgh Press Republican covered his six year boxing career extensively from 1951 until 1956–during which time he won five Golden Gloves Championships.

Ronnie was the ninth in a family of fourteen children. He was born in 1935, and by the time he was sixteen was already making a name for himself on the local Boys' Club boxing team, which sent it's best and brightest to the Golden

Gloves–sponsored by the Burlington Daily News Fund. In 1951, the Golden Gloves bouts were new, exciting and drew a lot of attention from the local populace and newspaper. Ronnie was a star athlete, and family history has it that he forged his mother's name on his first application to fight, as he wasn't quite thirteen at the time, the minimal age to get into the ring at the Boys' Club.

Ronnie fought in the 135 lb division, and lost only one match during his career–the final Championship match of his rookie year, to an opponent he wrested the championship from the following year. In his debut Golden Gloves match in 1951, the referee was forced to stop the fight in the second round as Ronnie TKO'd his opponent, Dan Ryan.

As the season progressed, Ronnie TKO'd one opponent after another and was declared the "surprise package" of the Burlington Boys' Club team. By the time the finals came around, he was the odds on favorite to win his division–which he did–which also meant a trip to Lowell, Massachusetts for the team, and the semi-final matches in the New England Golden Gloves Tournament of Champions, where he again won his division and the first of his five Golden Gloves Champion medals.

Over the next five years Ronnie dominated the sport and the newspaper headlines when it came to Golden gloves reporting. By then he was the odds on favorite in the ring, and judging by the amount of coverage the newspaper gave him–both in and out of the ring a favorite of reporters.

In 1956, after spending five years as the Golden Gloves Champion in the 135 lb weight division in Vermont, Ronnie was finally given the chance he so long dreamed of, when he was approached by a professional manager, John DeJohn of Syracuse, New York. At the time DeJohn represented the World Welterweight Champion, Carmen Basilio. DeJohn lined up a professional debut fight in Rochester, New York, and began training Ronnie for his first pro bout. It was a promising debut fight with Ronnie scoring a knockout in the first round.

Ronnie came home after his debut pro bout to train for the next fight, scheduled to be held in New York City, where he had previously fought in the Golden Glove finals, in two weeks time. But, unfortunately, that fight was never to take place.

On December 16, 1956, two dead bodies were discovered in a vehicle at the Williston sandpit. One of the bodies identified was Ronnie Begins. The initial investigative report stated that both had been overcome by noxious fumes inside the car.

The whole state of Vermont was stunned by the tragic deaths. After the announcement the entire sports section of the Burlington Free Press was devoted to the life and career of Ronnie, including full page pictures, retrospectives of his five year champion career, and headlines that trumpeted the fact that in his entire Golden Gloves career he lost only one bout, and was never knocked off his feet.

Ronnie's funeral was of a kind rarely seen in Vermont. The Immaculate Conception Church in Williston was overflowing, and hundreds of people had to wait in the parking lot during the service. The funeral home saw the same outpouring, and extended the visiting hours to include the next day to accommodate all the people not admitted the first day.

In January, as the Golden Gloves season again got underway, William Loeb, publisher of The News and Director of the Burlington Daily News Fund, announced the creation of a special memorial trophy that would be given each year to the outstanding boxer of the season–the Ronnie Begins Memorial Trophy.

Ronnie's family still adores this young man who filled his life with triumphs and joys, laughter and such promise. To this day there are people in Vermont who remember his glory days as the most promising young boxer ever to come out of the Green Mountains. This young, handsome heartbreaker who entered the amateur spectacle six times at Memorial Auditorium, and in front of a capacity crowd emerged as champion five times.

"Just Call Me Cowboy" Charlotte's Hugh Lewis, Sr.
by James Lawrence

First appeared in the March 3, 1994 issue of Charlotte News
Edited by Bob Winker

Bernie Cummings (right) and Cowboy Lewis (left).

There are older Vermonters who will tell you that the single greatest moment in the history of Burlington's Memorial Auditorium did not occur during any of the highly acclaimed performances of big-name musical stars who have graced its stage. It was not, they would say, the renowned appearance of rock legend Stevie Rae Vaughn, nor was it the brilliance of classical cellist Yo-Yo Ma. It wasn't Bob Dylan, Jimmy Cliff or even K.D. Lang. No, they will tell you, it happened one improbable night in 1956 when a pale-chest farm boy from Charlotte faced a would be world class boxer named Alonzo Moore.

It was billed as a classic Goliath versus Underdog match, with Moore wearing big league satin fighting robes proclaiming himself the "Next Middleweight Champion of the World" and going through a dazzling warm-up punching routine that might have put Muhammed Ali to shame. A big, strong, stylish fighter from Plattsburgh Air Force Base, Moore was clearly from the same mold as some of the country's great African-American boxers, and there was little doubt that he took the fight game very seriously.

In the opposite corner stood an unpolished, native-born Vermonter, a youthful 28 year old, and, if you happened to be close enough to notice, carrying with him the faint aroma of barn. At five feet, eleven inches tall and 160 pounds, the local boy, Hugh Lewis, looked like the sentimental favorite who was about to get his first major league comeuppance.

He wore a cowboy hat, an infectious grin and carried a streak of mischief into the ring. Eyeing Moore going through his theatrical shadow boxing routine, Lewis began to mimic the exaggerated motions of his opponent—much to the delight of the crowd.

What happened next was one of those electrifying, wholly unexpected moments that form lifelong freeze frame images in the minds of sports fans: Cowboy Lewis, as the Vermonter was billed, catapulted out of his corner. With neither fanfare nor much further ado, he planted himself squarely in front of Moore and, without a moment's hesitation, landed an awesome haymaker that seemed to come out of nowhere and straight into the face of his heavily favored opponent. As if struck by a horizontal bolt of lightning, Moore was stretched out flat on his back, dazed and, by all rights, defeated.

It was an incredulous moment for the 3,200 fans that had come to root for the homegrown underdog, and the capacity crowd jamming Memorial Auditorium to its rafters was on its feet. It was a magical, unpredicted upset, a Green Mountain farmer putting the would be world champion onto the canvas so decisively the referee seemed to be jumping in to stop the fight.

"I've never seen anything like it," said Bernie Cummings, for more than 20 years the Boxing Commissioner of the State of Vermont and himself a legend in New England boxing circles. "I thought the roof of Memorial Auditorium was going to blow off. I've never seen a crowd react to a punch the way they did to that one. You've never heard anything like it."

"The greatest show in the history of the amateur tournament" was the description used in the next day's paper by sports columnist Tom McCormick.

As it happened, the fight was literally over before it began: the referee said that the two boxers had come at each other before anyone could even sound an opening bell. The match had to be restarted.

Cummings said that Alonzo Moore, after some much needed recovery time, returned with new-found respect for Lewis, kept him at arm's length and neatly defeated him with superior technical boxing skills. Lewis readily admitted that he wasn't a scientific boxer.

In typical fashion, the defeated Lewis bounded to his opponent's corner after the decision had been announced to give Moore a congratulatory handshake and hug. He then sprang out of the ring–right over the top of the ropes–the exuberant way he had come in.

"If Vermont had a Boxing Hall of Fame, Cowboy Lewis might not be remembered as one of the greatest boxers," said Commissioner Cummings, "but he was probably the best showman I've ever seen. The crowds loved him. He had a tremendous sense of sportsmanship. And he was strong. If Cowboy Lewis hit you, you knew you'd been hit."

In 1950, he married Arline Mae Botala, whom he had met while haying at the Webb Estate in Shelburne, and soon embarked on a ten year career in the ring that gave him his colorful reputation. "I heard they were looking for boxers in Burlington, and I thought I might be able to make some money to educate my kids."

According to Bernie Cummings, Cowboy Lewis was one of a number of young local men who were attracted to the new Golden Gloves amateur boxing program that had been started in the wake of World War II. He remembered the day Cowboy appeared on his doorstep at the Burlington Boys' Club.

"He wasn't a fighter," Bernie recalled. "He was a farmer and he smelled like one–even after a fight and shower, he would still smell like a farmer because it was in his clothes. He didn't really know a thing about boxing at first, but he was strong, and a tough son of a gun."

Cowboy recalled the first time he got into the ring, he stood straight up and wide-eyed with his hands too low and wide apart. He promptly got clobbered, and as he picked himself off the canvas, began to appreciate the need for some training. Pictures from the era show a remarkable young Lewis with jet-black hair and an intensity that he's never lost. Cummings said that as Cowboy became known in local Golden Gloves competitions, his good looks "created quite a following among the girls."

His plucky character and ring antics made him a favorite with the crowds, as he blithely bounced over the ropes, repeatedly springing in and out of the ring, in what became his trademark entrance and exit. But he was a natural born scrapper, with an awesome punch that was respected far and wide.

The best fight of his career was against Leon "Skinhead" Liberty in 1955. Skinhead was a tough kid from the old North End, and they just stood toe to toe for three rounds, throwing haymakers at each other, which Cowboy won by decision.

As a Golden Gloves competitor, Cowboy was sponsored by H.P. Hood, with Clement Perkins as his trainer, and later by Sears, Roebuck with Al Reyes. Other managers who worked with Cowboy included Gene Couture, Emile du Pont and Luther Bridgman. Cowboy's showings in the Golden Gloves from 1950 to 1960 were always respectable, but he never went all the way. Sports Editor Rick Marcotte, writing for The Vermont Sunday News, called Hugh Lewis "the most popular fighter in the 1955 Golden Gloves Tournament." That year, Cowboy also represented Vermont in the New England Tournament in Lowell, Massachusetts.

"There never was a fighter that the crowds loved as much as Cowboy," said Cummings of the heyday of boxing in Vermont.

1953
Ralph "Tommy" Garrow – Rutland's Best
"I can't remember, but I won more than I lost"

Ralph "Tommy" Garrow

Tommy Garrow won the Vermont Golden Gloves Championship in 1953 at 147 lbs.; however, his boxing career started at age 7 when he boxed under the guidance of Crawford Taylor and Gary Matt, who trained junior boxers. Tom recalls that one year there were five junior champions on the street where he lived in Rutland. Between the age of 7 and 15 years old he won championships in the Silver Mittens and Junior Golden Gloves. By the time he entered the "gloves", he had plenty of ring experience–on a regular basis at the Mercury Club on Center Street in Rutland as well as in various towns in southern Vermont.

Tommy trained out of the Mercury Club along with his brother Jerry, Hank Miles, Jimmy McClarren and Bob Gale while preparing for the '53 Vermont Golden Gloves. He defeated Charlotte, Vermont's Hugh "Cowboy" Lewis for the Championship, but then lost in the New England Golden Gloves Tournament of Champions in Lowell, Massachusetts.

Tommy served his country in the United State Marine Corps, where he also had the opportunity to join the Marine Corps boxing team out of Quantico, Virginia. Some of his team mates were Terry Downs, Len Kestall, Richie Hill, Randy Horne and Phil Ortiz.

While living in Claremont, New Hampshire, Tommy won the 1958 New Hampshire Golden Gloves, as well as the New England Golden Gloves. Being the humble person that he was, when asked what his amateur record was he said–"I can't remember but I know I won more than I lost."

After numerous amateur bouts Tommy decided it was time to turn pro. His manager at the time was George Boland. Boland discovered "The Brockton Blockbuster" Rocky Marciano! While training out of Claremont and Ascutney, Vermont, his main sparring partner was Bob Gale, and a variety of boxers from the greater Boston area.

Tommy made his professional debut on April 21, 1958, in Providence, Rhode Island, as a lightweight. Tommy KO'd Tony Liquori of Agawam, Massachusetts, in round three of a four rounder. He went on to post a string of six wins until he faced a more experienced boxer in Johnny Bean of New York City, who KO'd Tommy in round five.

The highlight of Tommy's career came in January, 1959, when he won the New England Lightweight Championship. He had a record of 12 wins and 2 losses at the time he beat a much more experienced Tommy Tibbs of Boston, Massachusetts, in a 10 rounder at Acadia Ballroom in Providence, Rhode Island. In June, 1959, there was a rematch against Tibbs in which Garrow lost the title on a decision.

Tommy boxed at various venues throughout his career, including Madison Square Garden and the Boston Garden. His opponents included Paddy DeMarco, Joey Donovan, Iggy Maldonado, George Monroe, Pat McCoy,

Ralph "Tommy" Garrow after winning the New Hampshire Golden Gloves in 1958.

George "Kid" Ross, Lester Gonzalez and Bobby Veal. He quit professional boxing in 1960 with a record of 22 wins [14 KO's] and 6 losses. Explaining why he quit ahead of the game, Tommy explained that... "everyone was running my career except me! The venues were packed, but I got precious little out of it. My handlers wanted me to move to Brockton, Massachusetts, and train with Al Columbo, but I had a wife and two babies, and they wouldn't guarantee me a weekly income, so I quit."

As a boxer Tommy was something to watch. He had pure boxing form and wasted no punches. His opponent could throw 20 punches and..."Tommy would throw a right hand followed by a left hook, and often that was it!" said his number one fan, his wife, Marie.

Tommy never gave up boxing. He became a coach and trainer at the Rutland Boxing Club–later known as the Garrow Boxing Club. He trained 14 Vermont Golden Gloves Champions, and one New England Golden Gloves Champion–his son, Mark.

1954
Dick "The Moose" Greatorex
"One of the finest athletes to ever come out of St. Johnsbury."

1963 Vermont Golden Gloves Champions. Dick "The Moose" Greatorex far right.

They called Dick Greatorex–"Moose" or "The Great!" He made a name for himself both in the ring and on the football field. Dick was one of the best linemen to ever put on the pads for the St. Johnsbury Hilltoppers, and went on to star at the University of New Hampshire as well. While in college in 1960, Dick won the New Hampshire Golden Gloves, and then the Vermont and New England Golden Gloves Heavyweight Championship in 1962. He was one of the finest athletes to ever come out of St. Johnsbury, Vermont.

Dick got interested in boxing at the tender age of seventeen, and made his ring debut in the 1954 Vermont Golden Gloves. He fought Winooski native Ted Piche in the preliminary round and lost in the final round because of a cut. Greatorex then served in the Marine Corps from 1954 to 1957.

While attending the University of New Hampshire, Dick won the New Hampshire Golden Gloves Championship with three straight KOs. In his first appearance in the New England Golden Gloves Tournament of Champions, Jimmy Blythe stopped him with three seconds to go in the match. Blythe went on to the National Golden Gloves and was beaten in the finals by eventual heavyweight champion of the world, Cassius Clay.

In the 1962 Vermont Golden Gloves tournament, Dick won a unanimous decision over Bill Leahy, and the defeated five time Vermont Champion Paul Savage of Plattsburgh, New York. Reports have it that Greatorex had Savage on the canvas three times–twice in the second round and once in the third. He was able to hit Savage with vicious left hooks which stunned him in both rounds. In the New England Golden Gloves, Dick stopped Ken Jordan or Holyoke, Massachusetts, in the semi-finals, and the next night defeated defending New England Champion Cliff Savoy, weighing 278 lbs, of Manchester, New Hampshire in a unanimous decision. Dick suffered a broken nose in the fight with Savoy and was unable to compete in the National Championships in Chicago. In winning the New England Title, Dick was presented the Rocky Marciano Trophy, emblematic of the top heavyweight in New England. This was one trophy that the champ was very proud of, and displayed it in his living room at his Belvidere Street home for everyone to see.

Dick turned to the professional ranks in 1963, stopping Joey Lee of Boston, Massachusetts, at 2:43 of the first round in a bout in Rock Island, Quebec. Next, New England Heavyweight Champion Tom McNeeley of Medfield, Massachusetts, put his title on the line against Greatorex on February 12, 1966, at Boston Garden–in a scheduled 10 round match which Dick losts in the seventh via a TKO. BoxRec.com shows Dick having 11 pro fights from 1963-67, with seven wins (6 by KOs) and four losses–though it is fairly certain that he had more pro fights not recorded. Dick boxed in Boston Gardens, Madison Square Garden and the Montreal Forum.

The "Great One" not only excelled in the boxing ring but on the gridiron as well. While attending the University of New Hampshire he was on the varsity football team, and was a draft choice of the Green Bay Packers, and later signed a contract with the Pittsburgh Steelers–but several months later was released by the team due to an injury.

Dick trained mostly in the basement of his home, but during the week would travel to Derby Line to work out with Dr. Don Veeburst, and get some sparring in with other area boxers. On weekends he trekked to Burlington and worked out with the VFW team. He was always in shape and could be seen doing his road-work on the back roads of St. Johnsbury.

Richard A. Greatorex–"The Moose" / "The Great One" / "The Ox"– passed away at the Veterans Hospital in White River Junction on April 18, 1972, at age 37, suffering from a bout of cancer.

1954
Marcel Grimard

"It's time to get the street fighters off the street and into a gym."

Marcel Grimard

Marcel or "Marci" as he was called, got the urge to box at an early age–on the streets! Not as a street fighter but with other kids who had the same interest, boxing on the street where he lived in Barre. Later on they would all gather in his cellar for a sparring match. The cellar eventually didn't seem big enough so they moved to a larger building, a barn in Graniteville.

It was in 1968 that Grimard teamed up with Firpo Saldi and Gordon Grant–two excellent trainers–who were training boxers out of the National Guard Amory. "Marci" entered the Vermont Golden Gloves that year and boxed his way to the semi-finals in the 136 lb class, losing a decision to Patrick Malloy from Plattsburgh, New York. He also made it to the 1962 Golden Gloves semi-finals.

The year 1966 though, was "Marci's" year in the Vermont Golden Gloves. He moved up to the 147 lb weight class and won the championship, defeating James River. Not only did he win the championship, but he was also voted the "Outstanding Boxer" of the tournament. The award was presented by then Governor Phillip Hoff.

At some point due to work and lack of time to either box or train youngsters, Marcel decided to leave the sport. He was employed as an outside quarry manager at the Rock of Ages which frequently took him out of the area. Marcel also served over thirty nine years in the Vermont Army National Guard.

1955
Paul Savage
"A well traveled champion."

I had just knocked down Moose Gregory. The fight ended shortly after the knock down. I won by a TKO. Giving me the Vermont Golden Gloves Championship–Heavyweight that year.

Throughout Paul Savage's high school career, he was an outstanding athlete excelling in baseball and basketball at AuSable High School. During that time, 1951-53, AuSable won three consecutive New York State Section 7 titles, and Paul even received a try-out, and good scouting report with the Brooklyn Dodgers baseball organization. In 1955, at the age of nineteen, he became interested in boxing and joined the Plattsburgh Boys' Club Boxing team. His manager/trainer was ex-boxer Frankie DeCarlo who held training sessions at the Horicon Hose House (a vacated fire department building) in Plattsburgh. Plattsburgh had one of the best teams around in the 1950s and early 1960s. Paul also got help with his training routine from former heavyweight professional boxer Bob (Pastor) Pasternak, originally from New York City. Paul met Bob when he was working at the Plattsburgh Air Force Base. Bob would drop by the Horicon House from time to time to teach Paul how to throw different punches, work leverage and Paul's best strength. Bob had 65 professional fights, winning 53 (17 KOs), losing 7 and 5 draws. One of those losses was at the hands of Joe Louis at Briggs Stadium in Detroit, Michigan, for the World Heavyweight Title in 1939. Louis KO'd Pastor, "But that's no shame," recalled Paul, "...as not many boxers went the distance with Louis. I always appreciated Bob's help." Bob Pastor, born Robert E. Pasternak, passed away in 1996 at the age of 82.

Many fans packed Burlington Memorial Auditorium for the Vermont Golden Gloves Tournament throughout the years, and 1955 wasn't any different when Paul Savage entered the tournament with the Plattsburgh Boys Club. Paul would have to face many tough competitors to reach the finals each year. In 1955, he "decisioned" Winooski's Ted Piche in the semi-finals only to lose on a decision to Norm Fontaine in the finals, but returned to knock Norm out of the championship in 1956.

In 1957, Paul knocked out Jim Coleman in the semi-finals only to lose on a split decision to Bill Shepard in the finals. Shepard was injured in the match, so Paul represented Vermont in the New England Tournament of Champions in Lowell, Massachusetts. In 1958, Paul beat John Burton in the semi-finals on a decision, and then "decisioned" Hezakjah Marks in the finals. In 1960 and 1961, Paul knocked out "Moose" Gregory, and by a vote of the officials and the media he was named the Outstanding Boxer of the tournament.

In 1965, Paul was scheduled to box a Canadian boxer, Ray Coutier, in the semi final's—but Coutier was in a car accident on his way to Burlington and was unable to keep the match. When asked by the officials if he wanted a win by forfeit, Paul decided to fight both matches in the finals instead. He proceeded to beat Coutier with a decision in the semi-final, but then lost on a decision to John Goodrow for the championship in the final bout of the evening. That was the last of Paul's matches, with a very respectable record of 29 wins, 9 losses and one draw.

In 1961, Paul representing Vermont in the New England Golden Gloves Tournament of Champions in Lowell, Massachusetts, defeated Joe Hanlon and Jim Nizinski—and in so doing was awarded the prestigious Rocky Marciano trophy as the New England Heavyweight Champion. Throughout his boxing career Paul had tremendous fan support from his family and friends in AuSable Forks and upper New York State, as well as throughout Vermont. When he arrived home after winning the heavyweight championship there was a huge banner across Main Street in AuSable Forks that read "Welcome Home Champ!"

The next step on the tournament trail would be a trip to the Eastern United States Championships, where he represented New England. The event was held at Sunny Side Gardens in New York City. Paul met another tough boxer, Ray Patterson (younger brother of World Heavyweight Champion Floyd Patterson), losing a very close decision. Paul also won the Adirondack AAU Championship in the late 1950s, and in 1960 traveled to Ohio and boxed in the National AAU Championships. It was in Toldeo that he saw a tall light heavyweight (as an amateur), Cassius Clay–who won the National AAU title that year.

During the 1960s, Paul moved to Buffalo, New York and boxed at Memorial Auditorium–winning two out of three matches. Though he trained at Singers Gym, much of his training was done on his own–running, shadow boxing, heavy bag and speed bag routines. He was a well traveled champion, boxing throughout New York, New England, numerous other states including Ohio, as well as Canada. When asked why he gave up boxing, Paul replied that it was hard for him to stay in shape, because of a chronic knee problem that he'd sustained while playing baseball in 1951. He also didn't have adequate time to train properly. Paul married in 1961, and one his sons–Paul II–participated in the 1993 Vermont Golden Gloves.

In the late 1950s and early 1960s, Paul took up the sport of bobsledding at Lake Placid–starting as a driver and later switching to braking. He became a member of the 1964 USA Olympic Bobsled team–participating in the Winter Olympics in Innsbruck, Austria–and again in 1968, participating in the Winter Olympics in Grenoble, France. "We didn't win any medals, but gave 100%"–Paul later reflected. In 2004, Paul was inducted into the Lake Placid Hall of Fame.

Paul D. Savage, the best heavyweight champion to ever come out of northern New York. His name is mentioned frequently in conversations every year at the Vermont Golden Gloves tournament–a true champion and civic minded gentleman!

1957
Bobby Lefebvre, Sr.
"The Greatest Champion to Ever Come Out of the
State of Vermont"

Bobby Lefebvre, Sr., left, and Bobby Lefebvre, Jr., right.

Too small for basketball, and too light for football, Winooski's Bobby Lefebvre became one of Vermont's most famous and popular athletes. Coming from a poor family, Bobby shined shoes while in high school, but that would all change as his amateur boxing achievements became renowned. Boxing was his passion and he made the most of it! At 118 pounds he won many Vermont Golden Gloves, New England and New York AAU, and national championships. If there was a boxing tournament going on, that's where you'd find Bobby.

Bobby Lefebvre, Sr., right, and Bobby Lefebvre, Jr., left.

After winning the Vermont Golden Gloves and New England titles in 1957, Bobby moved up the ladder to the National Golden Gloves Tournament at Madison Square Garden, where he beat Howard Smith in the semi-finals, but then lost by decision in the championships.

In 1960, Bobby defeated Edgar Jones, the defending 1959 champion of Plattsburgh Air Force Base. By dethroning Jones and winning the championship, he was named the Tournaments Most Outstanding Boxer. Joining Bobby on the VFW team, coached by Leonard Sumner that year, was Allen Shangraw, Ronnie LaMarche and Skinhead Liberty.

Bobby had a brief professional boxing career in 1964, with a combined record of 3 wins, 2 losses and one draw.

Bobby revived boxing in the late 1960s and early 1970s throughout the state. He showed an interest in youth and boxing, and many clubs were formed bringing out former veteran boxers and champions who used their skills to train youngsters that wanted to get into the ring. These included Allen Shangraw, Jimmy Sheridan, Mike Armstrong, Claude Sheridan, Armand Gelineau, Rudy Loyola, Jimmy Forest and John McEnany–to name a few. Bobby had his own club and trained many youngsters including his sons, Bobby, Jr., and Billy, who went on to be champions in their own right.

Bobby went on to win numerous titles during his amateur career:

7 Time Vermont Golden Glove Champion

3 Time New England Golden Glove Champion

5 Time New England AAU Champion

7 Time New York State AAU Champion

4 Time National Golden Glove Champion

4 Gold Watches at Saratoga Springs Tournament

1957 National Golden Runner-Up at Madison Square Garden

1957 National AAU Gold Medal Champion held in Baltimore, Maryland

Total Record:

137 Matches

117 Victories (60 KO's)

17 defeats

3 Draws

Not bad for a little fellow out of Winooski!

Robert Leo (Bobby) Lefebvre, Sr., passed away on September 27, 2002. His friends, who affectionately knew him as "Mucker"–remembered Bobby as an avid outdoorsman, family man–with a real passion for the art of boxing.

1957
Harry Burdick
"The Crowd Pleaser"

Harry Burdick

Harry, from Hadley, New York, started boxing when he was seventeen under the watchful eye of trainer/coach Jim Monthony. When Harry stepped into the ring the crowd knew there was going to be plenty of action, as he was a "slam-banger" who could hurt his opponent with either hand. He participated in the Vermont Golden Gloves from 1957-59, and competed in the 126 and 135 lb classes in open division–winning three championships as well as a New England Golden Gloves title. In the mid-50s Harry faced the likes of Hank Miles, Joe Granger, Carl Bean, Jimmy Forest and Ronny Viau–the last three out of Burlington.

In the 1957 Vermont Golden Gloves 126 lb championship, it was Harry Burdick vs Claude Sheridan, who was boxing out of the St. Albans Club, who is now a retired dairy farmer from East Fairfield, Vermont. The following report was posted by the Burlington Daily News, and written by Al Bernadina. Round #1–Burdick opened fast and had the St. Albans lad on the defensive. A smashing right by Burdick of Corinth, New York, dropped Sheridan for an eight count. Sheridan was bleeding from the nose but finally gathered together an offense that shook up Burdick, but the rugged Burdick came back and staggered Sheridan. Round #2–Burdick was using the classic right cross and landed well to the head of the rugged Sheridan. Both of the fighters were slugging it out when out of the blue, Burdick landed with a right that KO'd the St. Albans representative. The time of the round was 2:11.

Harry defeated Burlington boxer Jimmy Forest (boxing out of the VFW Club) in 1958 and again in 1959 to lay claim to the Vermont Golden Gloves titles. In their first championship bout, the referee stopped the fight because Jimmy was bleeding from a bruise over his eye that he had suffered the previous week. There was even some doubt whether the ringside physician was even going to let Forest box that evening. Of course, Harry seeing that Jim had a cut–concentrated on that area, and it wasn't long before that cut was opened again. Once the ref saw the blood flowing, he stopped the match, awarding the championship to Harry.

The 1959 championship bout was slightly different. There was plenty of "slam-banging" between both pugilists. Harry could punch, but Jimmy Forest stayed with the flashy New York boxer for three rounds. Forest would side step Burdick and throw a barrage of left hooks. But Harry could hurt you with either hand and Jimmy knew that, so he would try to keep his distance whenever possible. It was three rounds of fast paced action. When the final bell rang, the Memorial Auditorium crowd was on their feet giving both a standing "O"–even though the crowd thought Forest had pulled out a victory. When the judges decision was announced that Harry Burdick had won the championship, the crowd couldn't believe it and started booing and stomping their feet. They truly believed that Forest should have won the fight.

1959
St. Albans Mr. Touchdown Ollie Dunlap

Ollie Dunlap (left) and Sugar Ray Leonard (right).

Go, Ollie, Go! came the chant from the crowds at Bellows Free Academy in northern Vermont. Mr. Touchdown, St. Albans Ollie Dunlap, started playing football as a sophomore in high school, and in just a few short years became a record setting senior averaging 29.6 points a game, and eventually leading BFA to two football state championships and one basketball state championship both in 1959.

It hadn't started out that way. Ollie and his five siblings arrived in St. Albans, Vermont, in 1956, following his father who was in the military and who worked at the radar station outside of town. The trail had been long as his family moved from Boloxi, Mississippi, then to Albuquerque, New Mexico, on to Spokane, Washington, and then to San Francisco, and finally to Vermont.

What Ollie did remember most from those early years in Vermont was how from the very start, the students and families at Bellows Free Academy immediately accepted him into the high school crowd. Faculty and staff also took note of the 6'1" student who would soon become an outstanding three-sport athlete.

On the first day that Ollie attended Bellows Free Academy, Chet Massa, Assistant Basketball and Head Baseball coach at BFA, approached him and encouraged Ollie to play. Ollie readily admits that he wasn't very good at basketball. He also did a stint on the track team which was encouraged by Coach Massa because he was not a very good baseball player. In his junior year in track, he won the 100 yard dash, the 220, and high-jump. He represented Vermont in the New England track meet.

In his senior year, Ollie won the 100 yard dash and high jump in the state, and represented Vermont in the New England track meet. He placed third in the New England high-jump. At BFA he played basketball for four years. In basketball during his senior year, BFA won the State and represented Vermont in the New England tournament. But it would be football that Ollie soon developed a passion for when he was approached by Bob White, head football and basketball coach at BFA. Ollie was also popular enough to be elected class president in both his freshman and sophomore years.

Ollie first tried out as a running back, and in his junior year, 1958, Bellows Free Academy won all their games and won the state championship. That year he was unanimously voted Vermont's all-state selection. The following year, 1959, the team again won the state championship, and Ollie was named First Team All American.

Ollie received numerous scholarship offers from Boston College, the University of Boston, Syracuse University and the University of Vermont. He decided eventually to go to Michigan State along with his friend Don Allard. But Ollie became restless at Michigan State and soon relocated to Toronto, Ontario, to play for the Continental Football League, and basketball for the Police League. It was there he met and married his wife, Linda.

Ollie eventually returned to football as a defenseman with the AFL [minor league] Toronto Rifles in 1966. He played in Montreal, Quebec, as well, but was soon traded to Hartford, Connecticut, where the coach, Tim Carpenter, a former running back of the Cleveland Browns, became assistant coach with the Washington Redskins: Ollie was drafted by the Washington Redskins on Tim Carpenter recommendation. Players on the team at that time were Sonny Jurgenson, Larry Brown, Bobby Mitchell, and Charlie Taylor.

While in high school, Vince Lombardi who was at that time assistant coach with the New York Giants, trained in Winooski, and that's where Ollie met Vince. After his release from the Washington Redskins in 1969, Ollie was doing volunteer work with the University of Maryland in their Special Olympics Program. It was there that he met Vince Lombardi's wife who was very instrumental in securing his position with Parks and Recreation in Maryland.

If you're wondering how this all relates to boxing and how a star athlete from St. Albans, Vermont, would become well known in boxing circles, the answer is in the likes of Sugar Ray Leonard and his brother, Roger Leonard. It was Roger, who around 1970, asked to have boxing lessons down in the Palmer Park Community Center. Two neighborhood residents, Dave Jacobs and Jose Correa, were volunteer trainers at the time. Because this was a self-sustaining program, money was tight. Teams in the surrounding neighborhoods didn't have a place to train either, so soon the Palmer Park Boxing Team came into existence. That is where Ollie met Sugar Ray Leonard, who lived three blocks from the community center. Being the excellent boxer that he was, Sugar Ray was a natural for boxing shows at the gym. When boxing shows were held at the community center, everybody came to see Sugar Ray, and by 1972, he was bringing home the trophies.

The 1976 Olympic try-outs were held in Vermont that year, and that's where the United States Olympic Boxing Team set up their training camp. A young Howard Cosell was at the opening ceremonies.

After a brilliant amateur career, Sugar Ray turned pro. During this time, Ollie acted as his administrative assistant, camp coordinator and media liaison [1980-1991]. Soon after, Sugar Ray retired from boxing. Ollie would go on to manage William Joppy who won the middle-weight world championship. Ollie also managed or co-managed several other boxers included Andrew Maynard, Lenny Stewart and Sean O'Sullivan–all gold medalists. Ollie retired from the boxing circuit in 1992, and still resides in Toronto.

1960
Brattleboro's Mike "Ace" Lucas

Mike "Ace" Lucas (left) and Angelo Iachetta (right).

Ace boxed in the Vermont AAU Tournament in the late 60's or early 70's at memorial auditorium in Burlington. He was a rough and tough boxer from Brattleboro who went through all competitors in his class winning the heavyweight championship. He was the talk of the tournament as nobody in this area had heard of him before the tournament. Ace then advanced to the regional AAU tournament in Troy, New York, and won that event as well.

Ace moved from Brattleboro to the Burlington area after the AAU event and participated in many boxing events around Vermont. He won many matches and was named the outstanding boxer in many of those. Ace would box anyone who wanted to step into the ring with him. Winning some and likewise losing a few along the way as well.

One of the more memorable matches I witnessed at memorial auditorium was the Harrison-Lucas brawl in 1973. Novice Dave Harrison of Burlington, a black belt karate expert, with no prior boxing experience, challenged Ace, a much seasoned open division boxer, to a match. Ace of course obliged. Who is the underdog in this one? Harrison, of course. Ace came out swinging and cut and dazed Harrison with a series of rights to the head and appeared headed for an early shower. Dave suddenly countered with left hooks which gained him the advantage in round one. Being the underdog, the crowd was on their feet urging Harrison to push forward. That he did and zeroed in on Lucas's jaw. Ace, as he has done in the past, dropped his hands and invited Harrison to attempt to hit him. Dave delivered smashing punches to Ace's head, earning the judges nod in round two. In round three, suddenly Lucas came on strong and was the aggressor but it was too little, too late as bartender turned boxer, Dave Harrison, went on to win the unanimous and popular decision. What a match. Never under estimate an underdog!

You will always find Ace at the annual Vermont Golden Gloves Tournament. I had the chance to talk with the veteran boxer recently and posed the question: Ace how many bouts have you had? "I've had 300 bouts. I started boxing as a youngster in the Lowell, Massachusetts, area." He couldn't remember what his record was.

In his latter years in the ring, Ace could be seen dropping his hands and telling his opponent to give me your best shot. The opponent would accommodate the offer and sometimes the outcome wasn't to Ace's liking.

It was 1977 when Ace ventured into the professional world of boxing and met eventual heavyweight champion Trevor Berbick. Berbick was born in Jamaica and made his home in Montreal. He beat Muhammad Ali in 1981, winning a unanimous 12 round decision. Well, Ace took the offer to box Berbick in Nova Scotia and this would be Trevor's third match as a pro. The match lasted two rounds and according to Ace, Berbick butted him, opening a cut, and the ref stopped the fight.

Ace is still in good shape and looks like he could still get into the ring and give anyone a good tussle.

The Glory Years: 1961-1964 Plattsburgh, New York
History Worth Repeating 1997-2008
MEW Press International

For a handful of years between the late 1950s and early 1960s, the Vermont Golden Gloves saw a flurry of spirited competition between competing boxing clubs around the compass from Lake Champlain, and fistic rivalries between Vermont, Quebec, New York and New Hampshire boxers, was the order of the day. At stake were not only individual championships but team titles. Still under the auspices of the Amateur Athletic Union, the desire to compete, and win, was contagious. From Paul Savage to Andy Anderson, Donato Paduano to Mike Armstrong, the packed crowds at Memorial Auditorium in Burlington where brought to their feet to cheer as hometown favorites displayed feats of fistic stamina and courage.

Plattsburgh was no stranger to the boxing life. In the late 1940s, Frankie DeCarlo began advertising for boxers to compete in Troy, New York. Within a handful of years, aspiring boxers from the Plattsburgh Boys' Club, Plattsburgh Air Force Base and the Plattsburgh Police Athletic Club were honing their skills at the Horicon Engine and Hose Company, and base gym to compete in the Vermont Golden Gloves. It might indeed be history worth repeating.

Vermont Golden Gloves 1961
112 lbs: Leonard Popcorn Smallacombe [Plattsburgh] vs
Kenneth Lafave [Altona, New York]

118 lbs: Bobby Lefebvre [Split Decision: defending champ, Burlington VFW] vs Maurice Mo LaFrance [New England Champ]

126 lbs: Ronnie Garrow [Plattsburgh: received Sportsmanship Award] vs Pete Lavallee [Burlington VFW]

135 lbs: Allen Shangraw [Burlington VFW] and six time 126 lb champ vs Bob Smart [Plattsburgh]

147 lbs: Ron Viau [Burlington VFW] vs Tony Lavelle [Plattsburgh]

160 lbs: Frank Buddy Decarlo, Jr. [Plattsburgh, defending champion] vs Ronnie Haydon [Essex Junction High School]

175 lbs: Andy Anderson [TKO-1: Whitehall, New York Outstanding Open Division fighter] vs Bill Leahy [Plattsburgh]

Heavyweight: Paul Savage [TKO-3: Plattsburgh] vs
Crawford Moose Gregory [Burlington VFW]
Plattsburgh Press Republican, February 9-10, 1961

Vermont Golden Gloves 1962

112 lbs: Leonard Pop Smallacombe [Unanimous Decision: Plattsburgh Boy
Club] vs Jimmy Creedon [Plattsburgh Police Athletic Club]

126 lbs: Pete Lavallee [TKO-2: Burlington VFW] vs
Ronnie Garrow [Plattsburgh Boys' Club]

135 lbs: John Williams [TKO-1: Plattsburgh Air Force Base] vs
Bobby Smart [Plattsburgh Boys' Club]

160 lbs: Buddy Decarlo [retains Middleweight title on a withdrawal: Plattsburgh
Boys' Club] vs Al Drink [Injured hand: Plattsburgh Air Force Base]

175 lbs: Larry Singleton [Outstanding Open Division fighter, TKO-2:
Plattsburgh Air Force Base] vs Andy Anderson [Whitehall, New York]

Heavyweight: Dick Greatorex [Unanimous Decision: St. Johnsbury, Vermont and
former New Hampshire Champion] vs Paul Savage [Ausable Forks, New York]

Novice Division Titles

118 lbs: Ken LaFord [by default: Altona, New York] vs
Frances Shover [Morrisville, Vermont]

126 lbs: Ron Murray [Unanimous Decision: Burlington VFW] vs
Ron Garrow [Plattsburgh Boys Club]

135 lbs: Ron Bezio [Unanimous Decision: Whitehall, New York] vs
Tom Weightman [Plattsburgh Police Athletic Club]

147 lbs: Johnny Pellerin [Unanimous Decision: Rutland, Vermont] vs
Gaylord McDonald [Altona, New York]

160 lbs: Mel Bushey [TKO: Plattsburgh Police Athletic Club] vs
Herb Cogston [St. Albans, Vermont]

175 lbs: Lloyd Yancey [TKO: Plattsburgh Police Athletic Club] vs
John Hylburt [Newport, Vermont]

Heavyweight: Howard Gero [KO-2: Plattsburgh Police Athleltic Club] vs
Joe Cota [Burlington VFW]
Plattsburgh Press Republican, February 9, 1962

Vermont Golden Gloves 1963
Novice Division
118 lbs: John Weightman [took crown: Plattsburgh Police Athletic Club]

126 lbs: Gary Garrow [Decision: Plattsburgh Boys' Club] vs
Wayne Moffatt [Morrisonville, New York]

135 lbs: Rogert Bovat [KO-2] David Lamos [Waterbury, Vermont]

147 lbs: Gaylord McDonald [Split Decision: Plattsburgh Police Athletic Club]
vs Adrian Despault [Waterbury, Vermont]

160 lbs: David McNeil [KO-1: Altona, New York] vs
Arnold Bocash [Morrisville,Vermont]

Open Class
112 lbs: Maurice Moe LaFrance [Win: Burlington] vs
Leonard Pops Smallacombe [Sportsmanship Award: Plattsburgh Boys' Club:
would go on to represent Vermont at the New England finals
118 lbs division]

135 lbs: Harry Burdick [KO-3: Glens Falls, New York & Plattsburgh Boys'
Club] vs Rod Murray [Burlington]

147 lbs: Tony Lavelle [KO-1: Plattsburgh Police Athletic Club] vs
John Kasper [Burlington]

160 lbs: Bobby Smart [KO-1: Plattsburgh Boys' Club] vs
Joe Granger [Massena, New York]

Heavyweight: Dick Greatorex [St. Johnsbury] vs
Howard Gero [fighting windmill style: Altona, New York]

Fay Averill was the Plattsburgh Police Athletic Manager

**The Burlington VFW and Air National Guard won a contested Team
Championship: with 20 points.*

Plattsburgh Press Republican, February 15, 1963

Vermont Golden Gloves 1964

112 lbs: Moe LaFrance [KO-1: Winooski VFW] vs
Germaine Grenier [Montreal]

118 lbs: Len Pops Smallacombe [2nd round win: Plattsburgh] vs
John Weightman [Plattsburgh]

126 lbs: Bobby Lefebvre [Stopped in 3: Winooski VFW] vs
Torade Baldassarre [Montreal]

135 lbs: Ron Garrow [Unanimous Decision: Plattsburgh] vs
Ron Bezio [Winooski VFW]

147 lbs: John Pellerin [TKO-3: Rutland, Vermont] vs
Gary Muir [Winooski VFW]

160 lbs: Don Brown [Win: Montreal] vs
Sterry Leno [Barre, Vermont]

175 lbs: Dick Dildy [1st round win: Brooklyn & Plattsburgh Air Force Base]
vs Dave McNeil [Altona, New York]

Novice Heavyweight: Tom Quick [Outpointed: Plattsburgh Air Force Base]
vs Howard Gero [Altona, New York]

Plattsburgh Press Republican, February 14, 1964

1961
Allen Shangraw

The Best 126 & 135 lb Boxer in Vermont Golden Gloves History

From Left to Right: Ron LaMarche, Chub Begins, Bobby Lefebvre, Jim Forrest, Paul Allen, Allen Shangraw.

Allen started boxing for the Winooski VFW team at the young age of nineteen. About that time he would drive his brother to workouts at the Winooski club, so one night Allen decided to do some sparring with the local boxers, and was soon hooked on the sport. That was the start of an illustrious amateur boxing career for Allen.

He first boxed in the Vermont Golden Gloves in 1950. While the team traveled around the state putting on exhibition boxing shows, Allen was slowly learning that being a "boxer" had its advantages over being a slugger. Over the next few years he won two state championships at 126 lbs. In 1954, he took time off from boxing and started to train other boxers, but soon returned to the ring and won back-to-back state golden gloves championships in 1955 and 1956. Allen boxed for both the Burlington and Winooski VFW, and trained under the watchful eye of Emile Dupont. A tireless boxer, always in great shape, Allen was a boxer with plenty of finesse–but could also "slug it out" with the best.

Through his eleven years of boxing, Allen had a record of 75 wins, 10 losses and 3 draws. For a kid that didn't participate at Burlington High School because of his size, Allen eventually won eight Vermont Golden Gloves titles and one New England title as well. He was also runner-up in Lowell, Massachusetts, in 1959 and 1961, and won the 1961 New England AAU championship in Boston.

Allen Shangraw (right).

Allen stopped boxing in 1962–as he never had any intention of joining the professional ranks. At that point he devoted much of his time to training boxers for state as well as New England competition.

Working out of the Burlington Moose Club and in later years the Winooski Armory, Allen taught his boxers the basics–lead with the left, then come across with the right. "I could only teach them what to do, but they had to work hard to get into shape," Shangraw recalled. Two of his young stable of boxers–Al Parenteau of Newport and Rick Ward–went on to win state titles. Rick also went on to Lowell, Massachusetts, where he almost upset the reigning two year champion.

After a brief hiatus, the Vermont Golden Gloves tournament was revived in 1977, and boxing has flourished in the state ever since with more boxers and boxing clubs than ever before. Allen trained and coached some excellent boxers through those years. To mention a few: Billy and Bobby Lefebvre, Jr., John Wood, John Cooley, Rick, Allen and Gary Ward, Ron Shangraw [Allen's nephew], Brad Cunningham, Brian Center, Billy Sweet, Dave Bergeron,

Tim Hackett, Kincaid Deforge, Gary Balcall, John Wells and Gary Valway–as well as many others over the years.

One boxer that Allen trained was Rick Gaignard from Ludlow. Rick was a student at the University of Vermont at the time he took up boxing. An excellent heavyweight, he was the only boxer in local knowledge to defeat Tony Robitaille in the Vermont Golden Gloves. It was Tony's first year in the gloves when the two boxed for the heavyweight championship, with Rick winning a close decision. Tony went on to win four successive New England Golden Gloves titles, boxed in the National Golden Gloves and AAU Tournaments, and was ranked as high as #2 nationally.

Allen retired in 1985 from the Vermont Army National Guard with 34 years of service. Along with his illustrious boxing career, Allen is a "heck" of a golfer. You might find him playing the game he loves any week with his golfing partner Bernie Rivers.

Excerpts included from an article by retired sports editor Don Fillion [Burlington Free Press] January, 1977.

1964
Mike Armstrong
"My only boxing regret was converting to a right handed boxer after winning the New England Golden Gloves"

Mike Armstrong (left).

Mike Armstrong (left) and Moe LaFrance (middle).

As a senior at Stamford Catholic High School in Connecticut in 1964, Mike entered the New York City Golden Gloves Tournament in the 147 lb class. With only one week of training, he won three matches before losing a close decision to the eventual finalist. But with no opportunities for boxing in his home town, it was the Vermont Golden Gloves that enticed Mike to choose St. Michael's College to further his education. The rest is history. Mike has been involved with amateur boxing since his years at St. Michael's–first as a boxer, then trainer-coach and as a USA Boxing certified official.

As a freshman at St. Michael's in 1965, Mike won the Vermont Golden Gloves 135 lb championship, and was voted the outstanding boxer of the tournament. With only eleven bouts on his record, he went on to the New England Tournament of Champions in Lowell, Massachusetts, defeating veteran boxer Walter Gavain who had over 100 matches under his belt. Mike is the only boxer in the history of St. Michael's College to win the New England Golden Gloves.

In the summer of 1965, while working with professional manager Bob Melnick of Harry Wiley's gym in Harlem, Mike converted from a lefty to a right handed boxer. This was the same gym that boxing great "Sugar"

Ray Robinson trained out of. In the 1966 Vermont Golden Gloves, Mike suffered a loss to George Graham, National Canadian Champion. Graham went on to win the New England Golden Gloves and was voted the Outstanding Boxer of the event. This was the first time a Vermont team member had received this prestigious award. George boxed his way into the semi-finals of the National Golden Gloves tournament.

Not discouraged by his loss in the Vermont Golden Gloves, Mike went on to win the 1966 Adirondack, New York regional AAU championship at 139 lbs. However, he missed the National AAU championships in Highpoint, North Carolina due to a broken nose suffered in a tune-up match. After healing from the broken nose, Mike won the 1966 Diamond Belt championship in Massachusetts, defeating previously unbeaten AAU champion Billy Weeks.

Mike was disappointed upon returning to St. Michael's in the fall of 1966 only to find that the Golden Gloves had been discontinued. Boxing eventually returned in the 70s as AAU tournaments then briefly as the Golden Gloves. When the Golden Gloves returned in 1978 Mike was co-director of the tournament and was the head coach of the Vermont team at the New England Tournament.

The urge to compete once again struck Mike in 1979, when at the age 32 he returned to competition winning the Vermont Golden Gloves 147 lb championship. After a twelve year hiatus and winning the championship, he received further accolades when he was featured in Sport Illustrated "Faces in the Crowd." Mike also boxed in the 1980 and 1981 Vermont Golden Gloves at 139 lbs, losing in the finals on a split decision. Mike then went on to coach the Essex Boxing Club which produced four time New England Gold Gloves champion Tony Robitaille, and two time middleweight champion Dave Fields.

Mike's only boxing regrets was converting to a right handed boxer after winning the New England Golden Gloves, and having the Vermont Golden Gloves discontinued at a time when he was really developing into a complete fighter. If he had stayed a southpaw, he could have repeated as a New England champ, and had an outside shot at the National Championship. Mike turned down an offer to turn pro from Boston promoter Sam Silverman out of frustration over the lack of good training facilities in Vermont.

After graduating from St. Michael's, Mike went on to the University of Vermont, receiving an MBA degree, and becoming a successful real estate investor and realtor for Century 21 Jack Associates. Since 1985, Mike continues to find his way into the ring as Vermont's oldest active referee.

1966
Donato Paduano

"He had determination to win every time he stepped into the ring."

Donato Paduano. (Photo compliments of Donato Paduano.)

Donato was the 1966 Vermont Golden Gloves open division champion at 160 lbs and voted the "Outstanding Boxer" of the tournament. But there's more about this boxer from Montreal. He also had an impressive amateur record of 83 wins, 6 losses and one draw, and a professional boxing record of 44 wins, 10 losses and two draws. With lightning fast hands and the determination to win every time he stepped into the ring, the many Burlington fans came to know him as Donato Paduano.

With the urging of his brother, Donato started boxing in 1961 when he was thirteen, at the Italian Boxing Club in Montreal. He formed a bond with the very well known and respected trainer, Roger Larrivee. It was Roger who molded Donato into the boxer he turned out to be–one of the best in his weight class in Canada and the United States.

Donato's impressive amateur career included winning the 1966 Quebec Golden Gloves championship in the 165 lb class, and winning the Montreal Golden Gloves in 1967. Donato then fought his way onto the Canadian National Team, and boxed in the Pan American Games–losing to eventual world champion Victor Galendez, and winning the bronze medal. In 1968, he won the New York Golden Gloves championship in the 160 lb class. Donato also boxed in the Olympics with the Canadian team where he lost his first match.

That same year, 1968, Donato decided it was time to turn the amateur experience into a professional career. Still under the tutelage of Roger Larrivee, but now training at the N. Palestre Nationale, Paduano dropped down to the Welterweight class and won the Canadian Title beating Joey Durelle by an unanimous 12 round decision at the Montreal Forum in 1969.

With a pro career that spanned 56 fights, Donato boxed and beat many notables including Marcel Cerdan, Jr., Ferdinand Marcotte and Louis Rodriquez. He also lost to some very well known champions such as Emile Griffith and Ken Bucannan–both world champions. Paduano fought Emile Griffith in 1974 at the Montreal Forum, losing a 10 round decision. Donato now resides in Quebec.

1968
Jim Churchill
"When I knocked that guy out, you could hear switchblade knives opening in the audience."

Jim Churchill: Franklin County and Vermont's Best

Boxer-puncher or slugger, take your pick, Jim Churchill was all of that and a whole lot more! If you wanted to box, he could do that and if you wanted to stand there and slug with him he could do that too. Beware: whatever the opponent chose to do in the ring, they would come out on the losing end! Proof is in the record books with Jim compiling a very ambitious record of 46 wins, five losses and one draw. Along the way he won four Vermont Golden Gloves titles, 147 pounds, two at 165 pounds and one at 178 pounds, not bad for the youngster out of Swanton who really didn't start boxing until after serving four years in the U.S. Marine Corps including two tours in Vietnam.

Jim credits Father Zider a Catholic priest from the Swanton area and Mike Armstrong, a Vermont Golden Glove Champion and 1965 New England AAU Diamond Belt Champion with piquing his interest in boxing. Father Zider was working with troubled youngsters in the area and invited Mike to come up to the Swanton Youth Center. Mike was a senior at St. Michaels College, that was in 1968, and Jim was a senior at Swanton High School. Mike is the type of guy who was always talking boxing and I'm sure that was his topic of conversation with the youngsters. Jim weighed 200 pounds at the time but was an excellent athlete and excelled in basketball and baseball in high school. Well, Mike got Jim's interest in boxing and you might say the rest is all history.

U.S. Marine Corps First–Boxing Second

Even though Jim's interest in boxing started when he was a senior at Swanton High School he really had to wait four years before taking on the sport with "vim and vigor". He had already enlisted in the U.S. Marine Corps and was on his way to Paris Island, S.C., soon after graduation, for 13 weeks of intensive "boot camp" training. The Vietnam war was at its peak, so soon after "boot camp" Jim was on his way to the war zone. He spent two tours in Nam, eleven months the first tour, then came back to the states to attend Airborne-Ranger school. Then it was back to Vietnam for five more months. Jim was a well decorated Marine. While spending two tours in that war-torn country, he received three Purple Hearts (for injuries suffered) and the Bronze Star Medal. The Bronze Star was presented to Lance Corporal James E. Churchill, "For heroic achievement in connection with combat operations against the enemy in the Republic of Vietnam while serving as a Patrol Leader with Company B. Third Reconnaissance Battalion, Third Marine Division." Four years in the Marine Corps, honorably discharged, now it was time to go boxing!

Fighting continued, only this time it was in the ring!

Memorable Moments in the Ring

Jims only draw and one of his losses was in two special five round bouts with a fine Montreal boxer by the name of Lancelot Innis. He fought Innis to a draw at city hall in St. Albans, Vermont and then losing a split decision to him at the Olympic Boxing Club in Montreal. "I thought I beat him both times," said Churchill.

Sailor vs Marine

This was a well hyped match. It was in the mid-70's and for the middleweight championship of the Vermont Golden Gloves. Churchill, the Marine meets John Olsen the Navy veteran, and a student at Lyndon State College. Navy vs Marine or Marine vs Navy!! Hold on to your seats, this is going to be a match you don't want to miss! The crowd is going wild in anticipation of this one! Round one: Olsen the less experienced boxer, threw everything but the kitchen sink at Churchill, he was brawling but a wild left caught Jim flush on the chin, dropping him to the canvas. The crowd is on their feet! Churchill a little upset that Olsen dropped him, survives the first round. Round two: Olsen continues with his brawling tactics, but not for long. With about a minute gone in the round, Churchill lands a right hand to Olsen's mid section and then another right dropping Olsen to the canvas for the 10 count and the only KO in the championship matches. Jim was asked to comment on the match, "Marine KO's Sailor, what a great way to win a championship."

Glens Falls, New York

My good friend, Teamer Lazure, was holding an amateur show at the Knights of Columbus Hall and invited Jim over for a match with a guy by the name of Dowdell. Mike Armstrong and myself were in Jim's corner that night.

Armstrong got a little upset with the ref in the dressing room even before the match took place. Mike had heard that Dowdell was a real hard puncher and told the ref he was going to keep a close eye on this match and the ref should do the same. Words were exchanged! So much for that! Jim scored two standing eight counts and won a unanimous decision!

Quebec Golden Gloves

Jim's good friend, Dick Thompson, would take him to Montreal from time to time to train at the Olympic Boxing Club and was invited to enter the Quebec Golden Gloves. Jim boxed his way all the way to the finals. For the Quebec championship, Jim beat his opponent from pillar to post, and was the winner hands down! Jim knew he had won the championship! When the decision was announced the win went to his opponent! Not only was Jim and Dick upset but so were the fans. This decision was so unpopular, that the huge crowd at the Paul Sauve Arena, became unruly and started pelting items in the ring. They knew that Jim Churchill had won the Quebec Golden Gloves Championship!

Switchblades in Asbestos, Quebec

Jimmy Sheridan, of the Tri-Town Boxing Club, with his Quebec connection got Jim a match in Asbestos, P.Q. It was a match with a guy who was the leader of a local motorcycle gang. The bout didn't last long as Jim knocked his opponent out in the first round! When seeing their leader on the canvas, members of the gang were apparently a little upset! Jimmy (Sheridan) told Jim after the match, "when you knocked that guy out, I could hear switchblade knives opening up in the audience." Time to leave Dodge! This is a story that only the late Jimmy Sheridan could tell!

"My best fights were with Lancelot Innis, who to my knowledge, went on to represent Canada in the Olympics," said Jim. "My most memorable Golden Gloves match was winning the middleweight championship on February 14, 1977, against John Olsen. Toughest fighter, Lancelot Innis," he added. I beat Al Parenteau of Newport, for my first title as a welterweight, Willie Thomas of the Lamoille Boxing Club for my first middleweight title, John Olsen, second middleweight championship." For the light heavyweight title, Jim beat Joe Allard of the Lyn-J boxing club out of St. Johnsbury. Jim said, "My fight with Joe was very action packed. He was a tough but very decent man. He's the type of guy that could be anyone's best friend."

Jim Churchill newspaper article. (Courtesy of Hubert Bushey and Vermont Sunday News.)

Accolades

In talking with Jim, he said I couldn't have had the successful amateur career without plenty of help along the way. "I want to thank you Ernie for the matches you got me and the places you took me. I want to thank Mike Armstrong for the hours and hours spent sparring and training me. Jimmy Sheridan for all the effort and help he gave me and for all the places he took me. And a special thanks to Dick Thompson, no man can have a better friend than Dick, I want to thank him from the bottom of my heart." Jim added.

Still Fighting

Jim is now battling the effects of the Vietnam war and was diagnosed in 2000 with "agent orange" cancer in his thyroid. Agent orange was a de-foliate used by the U.S. government in the war. The cancer spread to his salivary glands which two of them were surgically removed, then to his neck and vocal cords and was nine months without a voice. In December 2005, a surgical procedure was done successfully that now allows him to speak normally. Jim also had a portion of his left lung removed. Jim as everyone knows was a physical fitness fanatic, and still is. He still works out and hikes seven days a week. As Jim says, "Cancer is like a bully on the school grounds, once you stand up to it, it doesn't scare you anymore."

Arizona Bound

Jim and his wife, Maggie, now make their home in Chino Valley, Arizona. They still have ties to Vermont and New England, with children and grandchildren in the area. Daughter Christine and children, Nicolas and Kiley, live in Maine, son Aaron lives in New Hampshire with son, Ebben James Churchill, son J.J. is in Arizona and Jim's youngest son, Cody, lives in Franklin, Vermont.

I've had the privilege of assisting in Jim's corner, in many of his matches, as well as traveling with him throughout Vermont, New York and Canada. There isn't a better person or Champion boxer around than Swanton's Jim Churchill!!

1973
William R. "Billy" Lefebvre, Sr.
"It was an experience I wanted to try [turning pro]"

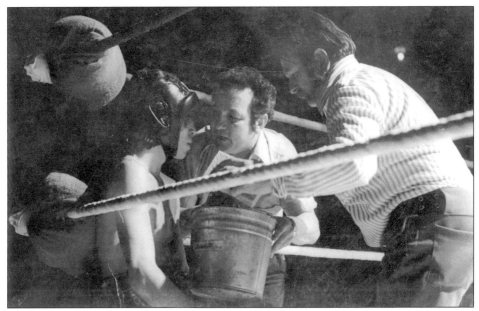

Boxer is Billy Lefebvre (left), Bobby Lefebvre, Sr. (middle), Jim Sheridan (right). February 5, 1974.

Not only was Billy a veteran of the ring but also a veteran of the military. He retired as a full-time Vermont Air National Guardsman on October 31, 2006. Senior Master Sergeant Lefebvre had over thirty years of service, which included tours in the war in Iraq.

The name of Lefebvre is synonymous with boxing in the state of Vermont. His father Bobby Lefebvre, Sr., was a many time Vermont and New England Golden Gloves Champion at 118 lbs. Then there was Bobby, Jr., who boxed at 118 and 125 lbs in the AAU's and the Vermont Golden Gloves. Then along came Bill, who carried on the Lefebvre family tradition of boxing following in his fathers and brothers footsteps.

Billy started boxing when he was sixteen years old, in the novice division of the AAU's (which his father brought to Vermont) during the revival of boxing in the state. Billy then moved up through the open class in the

Golden Gloves, and boxed in tournaments from 1973 through the early 1980s. He had some excellent trainers/coaches through the course of his career–his dad, Bobby, Sr., Moe LaFrance, Mike Armstrong, Jim Sheridan and Allen Shangraw. He boxed for the Burlington VFW Club, Burlington Moose Club, and in later years for the Tri-Town Boxing Club in Enosburg.

Along the way, boxing at 112 and 118 lbs, Billy faced some tough competition with many notable boxers including Mark Garrow from Rutland, Mike Robtoy and Ross Toof from St. Albans, and Danny Melendez of Maine.

Billy won the Vermont Golden Gloves championships through the course of his career, as well as boxing in the New England Golden Gloves Tournament of Champions in Lowell, Massachusetts. His amateur career ended in 1982 when he turned professional for one bout.

When asked why he turned professional, Billy remarked–"Jim Sheridan had taken a few of his boxers who wanted to turn pro to Canada, and at the last minute one of the boxers from our camp pulled out of the match, so I took the fight. It was an experience that I wanted to try." It was a six rounder in which Billy was ahead after three rounds, but the fourth round surprised him as his opponent was more experienced and knew how to conserve energy past three rounds. For his first and only pro fight, Billy was paid $200 Canadian. "Professional boxing is a lot different from the amateurs," Billy remarked. "No head gear, more rounds, more intense and "hell" with points!" When asked why he gave up competing in the ring–one word said it all–age!

But Billy never really gave up boxing after he left the ring competitively. He started the Bantam Boxing Club and has been training boxers for over twelve years–first out of the Winooski National Guard Armory, then at All American Fitness in South Burlington. He currently has a beautifully equipped gym on Malletts Bay Avenue–still called the Bantam Boxing Club.

Billy has trained many boxers through the years including his siblings, son's, Duane and Joey, and daughter, Melinda. Duane won the Vermont Golden Gloves in 1999, 2000 and 2001, and was runner-up in the New England Tournament of Champions in 2000. His career was brief with a record of 9-3 and 3. He's now a personal trainer. Joey was Vermont's first New England Golden Gloves Novice Champion.

Melinda started boxing in 1994 when there were very few female boxers in the sport. A petite lady weighing only about 95 lbs, she had to box girls 10-20 lbs heavier. She boxed in the Golden Gloves, but fought mostly exhibitions due to her weight against the likes of Stephanie Casavan and Tanya Morits. "I loved boxing as it was a great stress reliever, but I had to give up the sport when my youngster was born," she reflected. Now Melinda Travers, she resides in the Burlington area.

Billy loves getting into the ring and sparring with his pupils. Young and old, male and female, all train at his club–some will box, while others will train just to stay in shape.

Billy Lefebvre's amateur record stands at 40 wins, 10 losses and 3 draws, and in his brief pro career: 0-1, and he won the Vermont Golden Gloves Outstanding Manager/Trainer Award three out of five years. That's a record that speaks for itself! Billy currently lives in Underhill, Vermont.

1975
Dave Fields
"I started boxing for recreational fun–and a mean streak."

Tanya and David Fields, 1978 winner against Mark Fitzgerald. One trophy for the fight and the other trophy for Outstanding Boxer, Highgate Arena.

Dave started boxing at the age of eighteen and the young pugilist started training in 1975 under the watchful eyes of many times Vermont Golden Gloves Champion Allen Shangraw and Mike Armstrong. At that time local training space was limited, but Allen had access to the Winooski National Guard Armory to train boxers. Later, Dave took up training at an old barn in Williston. He eventually complied a very impressive record of 32 wins and 5 losses. When asked why he took up boxing, Dave remarked–"I started boxing for recreational fun, and a mean streak." Few though knew the Essex boxer as having a mean streak, except perhaps in the ring.

Dave's first four fights were in the AAU tournament at Memorial Auditorium (Burlington) in 1975 and 1976, where he won two and lost two in the 147 lb weight class. The Vermont Golden Gloves tournament had just returned after a two year hiatus, and started its new beginning at the Burlington Boys' Club–with a floor ring and a capacity of about two hundred. It took only one tournament to outgrow the Boys' Club, so it was moved to the Winooski High School, and then back again to Burlington's Memorial Auditorium, where it remains to this day.

From 1979 to 1981, Dave fought 31 bouts–claiming the 1979 Vermont Golden Glove Tournament runner-up prize in the160 lb weight class, as well as state Champion in 1980 and 1981 in the 156 lb class.

In 1981, Dave advanced to the finals of the New England Golden Gloves Tournament of Champions in Lowell, Massachusetts. He boxed a local kid by the name of Bobby Christakos. Bobby was an excellent fighter and perhaps he thought the kid from Vermont would be a push-over.

This was not to be. Dave pummeled Christakos, out-boxed him, and slugged him for three solid rounds of boxing. The local crowd was repeatedly on their feet giving Dave a standing "O"–they knew a good match when they saw one. Dave felt he had won the New England Championship, and so did the fans! Christakos knew he had lost–but not so! When it came to decision time, the Lowell area judges gave the decision to the local Bobby Christakos! It was possibly the worst decision ever witnessed at the New England Golden Gloves Tournament of Champions. Pandemonium immediately broke out at the Lowell Memorial Auditorium. The fans stomped their feet, yelling obscenities at the judges and tossing debris into the ring–paper cups, bottle caps, program booklets, anything a fan could pick up and toss into the ring. An intermission eventually had to be taken to clean up the debris and quiet the crowd with building Security in full force. It was a decision that would make any young boxer quit the sport, and it was–unfortunately–the last time Dave Fields was seen in the ring.

Reflecting on his amateur career, Dave mentions his best fight when he beat Canada's Junior Olympic champion at the Newport Municipal Building. His toughest match was in the 1981 Vermont Golden Gloves against a very tough local opponent, Mike Francis. It was three rounds of toe-to-toe boxing, and a decision that could have gone either way. Dave was able to pull out the win in the final minutes of the match. The worst loss, of course, was to Bobby Christakos in the finals of the New England Golden Gloves Tournament of Champions in 1981.

Dave also won the Northeast Kingdom Boxing Championship held in Hardwick, Vermont, in 1979 and 1980, in the 147 lb class. He faced some very tough competitors during his career including–John Terrell, Ed Petterson, Joe Allard, Mike Francis, Ken Alain, Clayton Mashtare, Alan Mashtare, Mark Fitzgerald and Dean Lambert.

Dave is a certified USA Boxing official, making his home in Underhill, Vermont.

1977
Elmer "Teamer" Lazure

"If a boxer was a student, every marking period they would have to bring their report card."

Tony Robitaille (left) and Teamer Lazure (right).

When Teamer left his professional boxing career, he didn't hang up the gloves–he started a new career training amateur boxers. Teamer was the best–not only did he make youth excellent boxers, but better students and citizens of the community. He trained boxers in Glens Falls, New York, and surrounding communities. Boxers from Vermont, as well as Canada, traveled to Glens Falls to seek his guidance and knowledge in the ring. Teamer was a no-nonsense straight forward trainer. If you wanted to learn the trade, he was always there to help. If you weren't serious about training, his Glens Falls Boxing Club was not the place for you. He took training and conditioning very seriously, and would not let a boxer enter competition until he was sure they were ready.

In 1977, Teamer invited a group of boxers from Vermont to one of his many amateur shows that he would promote in the Glens Falls area.Whenever he put on a show, it was always a packed house! Throughout the years, the Glens Falls Boxing Club had been part of the Vermont regional tournament, and after Teamer got the club up and running again, they had been invited back into the Vermont tournament. It was there that he met a young heavyweight, Tony Robitaille–a boxer with raw talent who trained with his brother, Robin. Robin was a good trainer who had brought Tony along as far as his knowledge would take him, so they sought out Teamer to give them some help. Every weekend they would travel to Glens Falls from Burlington to train under the guidance of Teamer. Teamer would eventually take Tony to some of the big tournaments around the country to get him more experience. Tony Robitaille went on to win four straight Vermont Golden Gloves titles, and four straight New England Golden Gloves Tournament of Champions titles. Tony also did an excellent job at the National Golden Gloves Championships, and won a spot on the USA Boxing Team–traveling to many foreign countries. USA Boxing ranked him as high as #2 heavyweight in the country. Tony knew that without Teamer's help and guidance, he won't have gone as far as he did in amateur boxing.

Other boxers who sought out Teamer's guidance of the "sweet science" included Floyd Peavy–who moved from Rochester, New York, to Glens Falls. Floyd went on to become a nationally ranked welterweight. He also won a Vermont Golden Gloves title and New England Golden Gloves Tournament of Champions title, and performed very well at the National Golden Gloves Championships. Young David Sibilou from the Montreal area was another very impressive amateur boxer, who's parents would put him on a bus and send him down to train with Teamer. Both Shawn Marcotte and Joe Allard (from St. Johnsbury, Vermont) and their trainer Victor Gammell would do likewise, a distance of nearly 200 miles. Gammell recalled that–"Not only would Teamer give my boxers advice on techniques of boxing, but would also teach me various techniques of training boxers. Going to the Glens Falls gym was always a learning experience." Both Marcotte and Allard had impressive amateur records and won Vermont and New England titles. These are just a few of the many boxers that would travel great distances to train under the guidance of Lazure.

If a boxer was a student, they would have to bring in their report card every marking period, to show that they were making progress in school. If they were failing a subject he would let them know that they should devote more time to their studies and should drop out of the club until they could bring their grades up. He didn't lose any youngsters because of poor grades–because they knew that Teamer was watching over them!

When youngsters in the Glens Falls area had a run-in with the law, namely fighting, a police or juvenile officer would bring them to visit Teamer. He would advise them in no uncertain terms, that if they wanted to fight they should learn how to box and do their fighting in the ring, not in the streets! He brought many youngsters who were on the "downward slide," back up to reality, and turned them not only into excellent boxers but better citizens.

Teamer was also very much involved with the Adirondack LBC, turning his garage into a gym to give boxers a place to train. He was also the head coach of the Vermont Golden Gloves team that won the team championship trophy in the 1986 New England Golden Gloves Tournament of Champions in Lowell, Massachusetts.

Reflecting on his own career, Lazure had 16 pro fights with 3 losses–the toughest being (where he was stopped on cuts) with Canadian George Chuvalo in Toronto. Chuvalo, eventually, went on to become the Canadian heavyweight champion. Teamers biggest pay day as a pro was $1,200 bucks. When asked who he considered the top three boxers to come out of the Glens Falls Gym, he quickly answered–"Heavyweight Tony Robitaille, Floyd Peavy at 147 lbs, and light heavyweight John Tyrell. Tony was the smartest boxer, and very easy to train because he would listen to you."

Elmer "Teamer" Lazure has done more for amateur boxing and the youth of not only his home town of Glens Falls, but the entire region. He deserves to be in the Boxing Hall of Fame! He was always a tough trainer–sometimes on the "gruff" side–but always had a soft and warm spot in his heart for our youth! He was the best!

James Joseph "Jimmy" Sheridan

James Sheridan

Jimmy's passion for the sport of boxing started at a very young age. Here was the promoter in him: he would encourage young fighters to spar and would then charge their classmates a penny to watch!

In 1954, he was crowned the Vermont Golden Gloves 118 pound Champion. Jimmy had received a bye in the opening round of the tournament and week later he scored a KO. For the championship Jim boxed, Jim Lester a scrappy high school student from Plattsburgh, New York. Lester the previous week had defeated defending champion Ted Germaine of Winooski. "Little Jim" from Fairfield is what they called him at the time and it took him only 1:20 of round one to dispose of young Lester. It was a barrage of lefts and rights that ended the hopes of Jim Lester. Sheridan trained under the watchful eye of Henry Gratton for six months, but the length of his boxing in Golden Gloves 1954 was only 3:12, which at the time was believed to be the shortest time to gain a championship in the tourney. On the same card that evening, Jim's brother Claude now of East Fairfield, lost a decision to Don Poirrier of Winooski. According to the Daily News, when Jim won the the championship, brother

James Sheridan (right) and Andrew Jordan (left).

Claude said "Jim is the best." Hugging his brother and with a smile Claude added "but I bet I can still lick you." At the time Jim and Claude were the only brothers in boxing. Unfortunately, Jim did not make the trip to Lowell, Massachusetts for the New England's as he came down with a severe case of pneumonia.

In 1972-73 Jim became heavily involved as a coach/trainer/promoter and was well known for coaching the Franklin County Boxing team and the Tri-Town Boxing Club. This also included coaching and training his two sons, Will and Dennis. He would promote local boxing shows and traveled throughout New England and Canada providing his boxers with many opportunities. Jim had several boxers that won Vermont Golden Gloves Championships and one boxer that went on to become a New England Golden Gloves Champion. Some of the outstanding boxers that Jimmy trained/coached include: Mike Robtoy, Ray Vallancourt, Randy Feeley, Jim Churchill, J.J. Bouchard, Clark Irons, George and Howard Britch, and Randy Corey, to name a few. There were many others. Jimmy received the Vermont Golden Gloves Manager/Trainer Award numerous times. Over the many years he coached, his boxers won Outstanding Boxer and Sportsmanship awards. The boxers he trained, their families and the many friends he had in the boxing community, were Jim's second family. Jim's heart was boxing and he truly was a fighter till the very end.

Jim loved people and was at his best when he was telling a joke or teasing someone to the point of an argument. With a wink of an eye he loved getting "something" started. There was nothing like Jim's laughter. He enjoyed gardening, taking care of his pets and was quite the cook in the kitchen. When it came to sports he was an avid Montreal Canadians hockey fan. And when it came to NASCAR racing, as far as he was concerned no one could beat #24 Jeff Gordon. Jim was also quite a pool player and won his share of tournaments in his younger days.

Jim's greatest love and what made him most proud was his family. He leaves his loving wife, Denise, and his children, John, Patti, Will, Dennis, and Kelly, along with their families.

We argued, we laughed and we had a lot of fun through the years. When Jim would call me, his first words were "what's cookin" and then the jokes, the taunting, and maybe a friendly argument before he hung up the phone. The boxing community needs more "Little Jim" Sheridans. We all miss you Jim, and I especially have lost a very close friend.

1977
Tony Robitaille
"They were playing politics with the pairings."

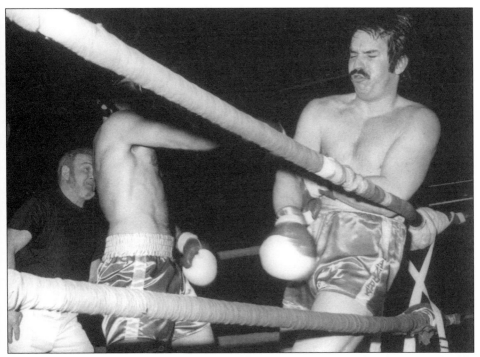

1979 Final Vermont Golden Gloves. Tony Robitaille (right) vs. Mark Landry of Maine. Robitaille wins by 1st round knock out. (Picture compliments of Tony Robitaille.)

Four time Vermont & New England Golden Gloves Heavyweight Champion: Tony Robitaille

Four consecutive Vermont Golden Gloves titles, four consecutive New England Golden Gloves Tournament of Champions titles, but wait there's more! Winner of four Rocky Marciano trophies, emblematic of the best heavyweight boxer in New England, Empire State games champion, traveled to Sweden with a New York City boxing team, winner of many outstanding boxer trophies and was ranked #2 in the country! Boxed Mike Tyson and Joe Louis! Not bad for a youngster out of Newport, Vermont, or as many refer to it as the "Northeast Kingdom" of Vermont.

Tony was a competitor all through high school competing on various sports teams out of North Country Union High School. In 1975, he won the shot put and discuss events in the state track and field championships. When he graduated from high school and went to work at Butterfields Tap & Die, now Tivoli's, he was lost without being active and able to compete. Al Parenteau suggested boxing and Tony thought that was a good idea so he started training in September, 1977, with Dr. Donald Veeburst at his Derby Line gym. Doc Veeburst was well recognized as an excellent trainer who had also trained professional boxers at his gym. His first bout was in December, 1977, in St. Johnsbury winning a unanimous decision over Rocky of Barre.

Then Came the Vermont Golden Gloves

In 1978, Tony boxed for the first time in a competitive and advancing tournament, "The Vermont Golden Gloves". He boxed his way into the finals losing a split decision to Rick Gaignard of Ludlow, who was then a student at the University of Vermont. It was a very close match that many thought Robitaille had won "I always wanted a re-match with Rick," said Tony, but that never came about for one reason or another. There was a trainer seated in the audience that night who saw great potential in the young boxer from Newport. Teamer Lazure of Glens Falls, New York. Glens Falls through the years had been part of the Vermont Golden Gloves but did not have a team entered in the tournament as it was the first year of the resurgence of the event. Tony and his brother Robin, who also trained the heavyweight, became good friends with Teamer. Both of them would travel to Glens Falls where Teamer would hone Tony's skills with excellent sparring and instruction. With Teamer and Robin, Tony would travel throughout New York and Vermont and other states boxing at various club shows and tournaments. Over next four years Tony was untouchable. Winning four Vermont and New England Golden Gloves titles. I can recall one match in the Vermont Golden Gloves when Tony fought a boxer out of the Gamache boxing club in Lewiston, Maine. It was Marc Landry who had boxed in the Army. Many thought this would be Tony's demise: a boxer with less experience going up against a more experienced competitor. It wasn't going to happen as Robitalle dropped Landry like a "sack of potatoes" in the second round. Landry never wanted to tangle with Tony again.

New England Golden Gloves Tournament of Champions, Lowell, Massachusetts

Tony was my first New England Golden Gloves Champion in 1979. He went toe to toe, a slugfest you might say, with Chris McDonald of Tiverton, Rhode Island, who was out of the Southern New England Golden Gloves. Chris was a real tough boxer. "I hit him with everything I had and he wouldn't go down, he must have a head made of "cement"," said Robitaille. Who did he face in the finals the following year? None other than Chris McDonald and again it was much the same type of bout as the previous year. Toe to toe from start to finsh. In 1981, Tony faced a huge, I mean a real big opponent in the finals of the New Englands. He was Harold Rice, "The Mountain Man" out of the Holyoke Boys' Club Golden Gloves. You can imagine a boxer a lot taller and heavier, maybe a hundred pounds heavier than Tony. Keep in mind, there wasn't a super heavyweight division, at this time so you boxed all opponents from 180 pounds on up. The sky was the limit. What a match that was, Tony

1980 Semi Final N.E. Golden Gloves, Lowell, Massachusetts. Tony Robitaille wins unanimous decision over Harold (Mountain Man) Rice of Holyoke, Massachusetts. (Photo compliments of Tony Robitaille.)

got inside of Rice and stayed there every round working the combinations to his advantage, winning on a decision. In 1982, Tony boxed a tough fight with Eric Hodges also out of the Holyoke Boys' Club. It was a blood bath as Hodges broke Tony's nose. This guy was quite the clown in the ring, sticking his tongue out and making all sorts of gestures and quite mouthy as well. He did receive warnings from the ref. In the end, broken nose and all, Tony got the decision. The sad part is that Tony had received an invitation to go to the Olympic Training Center in Colorado, but with the broken nose he was unable to attend and was also notable to compete in the National Golden Gloves Tournament of Champions.

In 1979 and 1981, Tony made it to the quarter-finals of the National Golden Gloves Tournament of Champions and in 1980, boxed his way into the semi-finals. The National Golden Gloves is held in a different city and state each year.

Snafu at the National AAU'S

Tony won the New England and Adirondack AAU regionals in Glens Falls, New York, and then travelled to San Francisco, California for the Nationals. The Amateur Athletic Union (AAU) was the forerunner of USA Boxing. He made it to the quarter-finals by beating Steve Singleton of the U.S. Navy boxing team on a split decision. For the second round, AAU officials changed the pairings, a change that Robitaille wasn't at all pleased with. He was scheduled to box Tyrone Biggs of Philadelphia, but when Tony arrived for the weigh-ins, he was notified of the change and would now box John Keyes of San Francisco. "They were playing politics with the pairings and wanted Biggs and Keyes in the finals," said Tony. I said, "The only way Tony is going to beat Keyes, was to put him on the floor." Robitaille received warnings in his bout with Keyes for putting his head on Keyes chest. Tony lost on a split decision

Robitaille meets "Iron" Mike Tyson

Teamer Lazure was good friends with the late Cus D'Amato from the Catskills. Cus was the trainer of many amateur boxers and professionals as well. Most notable for training heavyweight champion Floyd Patterson ... Teamer and Tony would travel to Cus's gym in the Catskills occasionally to get some sparring with other boxers. D'Amato had this young boxer from New York City he was training by the name of Mike Tyson. Tyson was only 14 or 15 years old at the time and a real powerhouse of a boxer. Tony was able to get a few sparring sessions in with him. "Every time Tony would start getting to Tyson, Cus would want to stop the session," said Lazure.

Cus invited Tony and Teamer to a club show he was holding in the Catskills. Teamer wanted Tony to box Tyson and Cus agreed. What a match it was! A real three round slugfest! Lazure said the first round went to Tyson, the second round was about even and in the third round Robitaille was all over Tyson. Tyson wins it on a split decision. Cus said, "Tony got robbed, it was a hometown decision." If Cus was alive today, he would tell you the same thing.

Even to this day when you tell people that Tony boxed Mike Tyson as an amateur, they can't believe it.

Other Tournaments

Tony won the Empire State Games in 1980 and also the Sugar Ray Leonard Golden Gloves. He also won a spot on the U.S.A. Boxing team and traveled to foreign countries to compete. Robitaille boxed throughout the region: Burlington; Glens Falls, New York; Catskills, New York; Albany, New York; Newport, Barton, Hardwick, St. Johnsbury, Springfield and Essex Junction. His last fight took place in his hometown of Newport in June, 1982, knocking out a boxer from Rochester, New York, by the name of Joe Louis! Ending his career the way he started in 1977 with a win and a record of 47 wins and 7 losses.

Decision Time

I posed the question: Why did you give up boxing? "I lost my desire to train hard and knew I either had to quit amateur boxing or go professional. My desire to retire was not easy but decided to do so. My gut feeling helped me decide to leave the sport and I will always wonder what kind of career I have had at the pro level," said Robitaille.

Tony had help in his successful amateur career from various trainers including Dr. Donald Veeburst, Dr. Dennis LeBlanc, Al Shangraw, Mike Armstrong and above all his brother, Robin. Robin started helping Tony train and was with him right up to the finish. Wherever Tony had a bout, Robin was always there. He had tremendous support from his entire family.

Tony now lives in Williston with his wife and children and is a driver for UPS.

I have been involved with amateur boxing for thirty years and to this day I have not seen a heavyweight in New England that could top this young boxer from Newport. Tony Robitaille was the best!

Joey Gamache, Maine's Best Boxer

Joey Gamache (left) and Emanuel Steward (right).

An amateur record of 86 wins and 12 losses. National Junior Olympic Champion in 1982. Three time Vermont and New England Golden Gloves Champion. Voted the Outstanding Boxer at the New England Golden Gloves Tournament of Champions. Runner-up in the National Golden Gloves Tournament of Champions in 1984. Earned a bronze medal in the 1984 Olympic trials. Traveled around the world with the USA Boxing Team. Just a few of his accomplishments as an amateur! Now, how about this: He turns professional in 1987 defeating Al Jackson via a tko in the fourth round in Lewiston, Maine. The rest is history. A pro career that spans 13 years and a record of 55 wins (KOs 38) lost 4 and no draws. He is also the first boxer from Maine to capture a World boxing title, winning the WBA lightweight title with a ninth round stoppage of Chil-Sung Chun in Portland, Maine, in June of 1992. Along the way he also won Junior lightweight titles.

Not bad for young Joey Gamache from Lewiston, Maine, who gave up playing little league baseball at the age of 10 to pursue a career in boxing.

His father Joe, Sr., had a gym and still does in Lewiston and that's where it all started. Joey trained under the watchful eye of his father and also Tony Lampron. Joe has trained some excellent boxers and has always brought a very strong team to the Vermont Golden Gloves. There was only one year since 1977 that Joe was unable to bring a team of boxers to Vermont. As you can imagine, young Joey would attend the gloves with his fathers boxing team and when he was around 13 years old would beg the tournament director to let him enter the gloves. Of course, he couldn't enter because of his age, but oh how he would beg. Everyone knew that Joey was an excellent boxer even at that tender age.

When Joey entered the Vermont Golden Gloves at age 16 he literally went through every opponent, not only in Vermont but Lowell, Massachusetts, as well. He was one heck of a boxer! Joey was asked recently to look back at some of the matches he had in Vermont and who was the toughest boxer he faced? "Sean Bradley," said Gamache. Sean Bradley from the Mashfield-Plainfield, Vermont area gave Joey one of his toughest matches. Bradley was a strong kid who trained under the guidance of Teamer Lazure from the Glens Falls Boxing Club. It was a pier six brawl! There wasn't a dull moment from the opening bell to the last. Joey found out in a hurry that Sean was not going to be a push-over as it was toe to toe all the way. Joey did pull out the win on a split decision.

Joey boxed in the 132 and 139 weight division in the Gloves and for most of his career. His nephew, Jeff Wright, also won a Vermont Golden Gloves title as well as his son, Steven Gamache.

Joey retired from the ring in February 2000 after suffering a concussion when knocked out by Arturo Gatti in Madison Square Garden. At this writing he is currently in litigation against Gattti and the New York State Athletic Commission in Manhattan Federal Court. The suit claims that Gamache suffered brain damage against Gatti, who Joey alleges weighed close to 160 pounds for a fight in which both participants were contracted to be 141 pounds eight hours prior to the match. What a ring career Joey has had, boxing the likes of championship caliber fighters as Julio Cesar Chavez, Tony "The Tiger" Lopez, Orzubec Nazarov and Arturo Gatti along the way.

Young Gamache has come full circle, first as an amateur, then professional and now a trainer of boxers. Some people in boxing circles say he is a "Teacher" of boxers. He has trained or taught boxers the sweet science at Gleasons Gym as well as the Fighthouse in New York City.

Joey is now training assistant or understudy for the legendary Emanuel Steward's ever growing stable. He says he couldn't be happier about his good fortune and the prospect of a future doing what he knows and loves best.

In the late 70's and into the 80's, Steward a National Golden Gloves champion in 1963, turned out world champions at Detroit's fabled Kronk Gym. Fighters like Tommy Heams, Hilmer Kenty, Jimmy Paul and Milt McCrory. Emanuel had them from the first day they entered the gym.

Gamache was originally recommended to Steward by well-traveled, longtime New York based cut man, Jimmy Glenn. As a joke Emanuel kept playing stupid, as if he didn't know who Gamache was. All the while, however, he was planning on bringing Joey onto his team.

"Emanuel takes nothing for granted," said Garnache. "Watch him in the corner. There is never any confusion. He has great composure and confidence, and he transfers that to his fighters. As far as I am concerned, when it comes to trainers, there is Emanuel and then there is everyone else."

Gamache has watched the steady progress of middleweight Andy Lee, cruiserweight Johnathan Banks and welterweight titlist Kermit Cintron. In the short time he has been working with Steward, he has seen those already accomplished fighters grow in leaps and bounds. He has spent time in Austria and Germany with IBF heavyweight champion Wladimir Klitschko and Kermit Cintron.

As much as he loves training, Joey says that being away from his wife Sissy so often has been difficult. Sissy, a Costa Rican native, is an actress who came to New York to follow her dreams. That's why she understands her husbands desire to follow his own dreams, even though they are now taking him around the world, very often on relatively short notice.

Steward feels as luck to be associated with Gamache as the other way around. "Unlike a lot of trainers, Joey is very low key," said Emanuel, "He wants to work hard and learn and he doesn't have his own agenda."

"Someone like Joey will develop into a real teacher. He was a great fighter and he's a great learner. But I've never heard him once say how great, or even how good he was. If he's in the gym three hours, he's working every minute. I have a lot of trust and faith in him. He deserves it," said Emanuel Steward. Knowing Joey all these years I agree with Emanuel!

(Some of the material for this story was taken from The New York Times, the sweetscience.com, fighthouse.com and Boxrec.com)

Duxbury's Champion Scott D. Patterson
In Memory
Vermont Golden Gloves "Outstanding Boxer Award"

Scott Patterson (right).

In 1985, Scott stepped onto the scales at Memorial Auditorium. Here is this young blonde, 16 years old, about to enter his first Vermont Golden Gloves tournament. "What's your name?" I asked, "Scott Pattterson of

Duxbury," he replied, with him was Joe Stone and the late Bob Dragon, both seasoned boxers who chimed in that this young 125 lb boxer is a tough competitor. Scott would travel from his home in Duxbury to train with the two veteran boxers at the Burlington Boys' Club. Opening nite of the 1985 "gloves" launched Scott on a very impressive amateur career. Keep in mind, there wasn't a novice class and depending how many entered a class, it wasn't unusual for a boxer to have two matches in one night. Scott boxed his way to the championship round in 1985 and 1986 losing on a decision both years.

Scott was a student at Harwood Union High School and it was difficult for him to make the trip to Burlington to train at the Boys' Club. His father, Ed, built a gym in a barn behind their house and named it "The K-O Boxing Club". It wasn't long before word got around that there was a gym in town, and the club grew to 12 boxers. Ed took over training his son with the watchful eye of Scott's grandfather, Jack, who also boxed in the 1940's. In 1990, the club entered 10 boxers in the Vermont Golden Gloves and ended with 7 champions and 3 New England runners-up.

In 1987, Scott moved up to the 132 lb weight class and went on to win four Vermont Golden Gloves championships in that class. He was a four time New England Golden Glove runner-up. Scott would tell you he got robbed of the decision in two out of the four years and should have been a two time New England Champion.

Scott, with his dad as his trainer/coach, travelled extensively throughout New England, New York, Quebec participating in every boxing event possible. He even trained for awhile with John Scully, a New England Champion who went on to box professionally. In 1989, Scott was invited to participate in a two week intensive Olympic Boxing Training in Lake Placid, New York. In 1989 and 1990, he was named Amateur Athlete of the week by the Washington World newspaper in Barre.

The young boxer from Duxbury ended his career with 39 wins and 8 losses. He lost only twice in Vermont. Four New England losses, lost a split decision to Shawn Powell and lost to Tony Marshall of Troy, New York, on an injury from a low blow and could not continue. Tony went on to become a champion in the professional ranks.

One of the matches that comes to mind was the bout he had with Joe Aliot at the New England Golden Gloves Tournament of Champions in Lowell, Massachusetts. Aliot was with the Lowell team. Scott literally beat him from

Scott Patterson (right).

"pillar to post" in every round. The crowd was on their feet for this one. The young lad from Vermont was beating a hometown favorite. When the bout ended, the crowd was still on their feet with a standing "'O". Everyone knew that Scott had won this one. But wait, when the results were announced the judges gave the decision to Aliot! Fight fans could not believe this one! They knew young Patterson had won the bout and the judges were showing favoritism towards a Lowell boxer.

There was another instance in Somerville, Massachusetts, when Scott totally outboxed a local opponent. The crowd knew that Scott had won the match but the judges didn't see it this way and gave the bout to the local boxer. Not only were the fans in the stands upset with the decision but so was his father, Ed, and his uncle, David. David went to ringside and argued with the judges on this one. It didn't do any good arguing the results, in fact, officials went so far as wanting David tossed out of the auditorium!

After leaving boxing Scott became a police officer, first with the Waterbury Police Department, then the Washington County Sheriff's Department and later for the Hartford Police Department While serving in Waterbury, Scott founded the Neighborhood Watch program and a K-9 unit. In 1999, a German Shepherd named Jerry Lee became Scotts best friend and partner in solving crimes. Scott was also presented the prestigious Legion Heroism Award by the Vermont American Legion, for his work in law enforcement.

Scott D. Patterson, at age 34, passed away unexpectedly at his home in Berlin on January 18th, 2003, leaving his wife Jennifer and two children, Emily and Trevor, and his beloved partner, Jerry Lee. He also leaves his mom and dad, Ed and Maureen of Duxbury, and his brother, Mark, of Tennessee.

Whenever Scott was off duty from law enforcement and able to go to the gloves, he would always come to me and shake my hand and remind me that if I had any problems he was there to help. I always appreciated that.

Rutland's Cal "The Barber" Josselyn

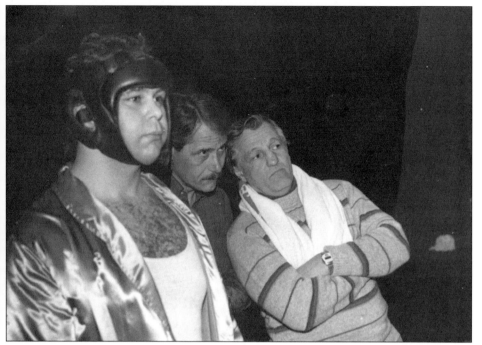

Cal Josselyn, Jr., (fighter), Cal Josseslyn, Sr., (middle) and Tommy Garrow (trainer). 1987.

Two weeks before the 1986 Vermont Golden Gloves tournament, Cal Josselyn started training with Tommy Garrow. Tommy though, never allowed any of his boxers to enter an event unless they were ready and on the "top of their game." So, Cal had to wait and continue his training, while picking up a couple of bouts during the summer and fall of that year, and eventually going on to win the 1987 Vermont Golden Gloves Heavyweight Championship–defeating Bakerfield's Clarence Williams. Cal then boxed his way into the finals of the New England Gold Gloves Tournament of Champions, losing a tough split decision to George Brice of the Holyoke Boys' Club.

Following that loss in Lowell, Massachusetts, Cal went home, got married and settled down. Working three jobs left him little time to train, but he did manage to take in some club bouts, or "smokers" as they were called.

After a years absence from the ring, and with the Rocky Marciano Trophy [presented to the heavyweight champion of the New England Golden Gloves Tournament of Champions] as his goal, Cal lost weight and entered the 1989 Vermont Golden Gloves, where he won the heavyweight championship defeating Jim Giroux. In Lowell, he boxed his way into the finals but lost on a split decision to Don Beech of the Holyoke Boys' Club. Over his short [some 15 to 20 fights] boxing career, Cal only remembers one other loss–to Corey Coulter of the Hoosick Falls, New York, boxing club. After that fight, Don Hamilton, who coached the Hoosick Club, presented Cal with the trophy because he felt he had actually won the fight. Cal later defeated Coulter on his way to the championship in the 1989 Vermont Golden Gloves.

Cal's training in the gym through his short but successful career included sparring with over fifty different boxers including the Shattuck brothers, Jim Raybourne, Bill Kelly, Angello Iachetta and Steve Walker. After retiring from the ring, Cal assisted Tommy Garrow in training boxers. He also went on to personally train one Golden Gloves champion, Darrel Alberico, and one Tough Man champion, Mike "The Beast" Bevins. Cal kept busy refereeing pro fights in Rutland, as well as Tough Man contests throughout Vermont, New Hampshire and Maine. Cal, Jr., and his father, own "Cal's Hair Associates" on State Street in Rutland.

Cal is a giant of a person with a big heart, and was an excellent heavyweight champion!

1986
Jeff Batchelder
"My Life with the Gloves"

Jeff Batchelder

My Interest in Boxing

My first introduction to boxing was in 1982. I had watched boxing on television and knew then I wanted to become a boxer. Bob Wright, who lived in my hometown of Greenwich, New York, opened a boxing club in the basement of the town's community center. The gym had been opened for about six months when I started training there. After about a month from the time I joined the club, it suddenly closed down. Now I was in search of another club.

In 1984, I discovered the Hoosick Falls, New York, boxing club operating out of the National Guard Armory. Don Hamilton was the trainer/coach and he was training a lot of good boxers there. I decided that was the club to join. My brother Dan was only six years old when he started going to the gym with me. I was fifteen at the time.

My first boxing match was December 8th, 1984, at the Catamount School in Bennington, Vermont. I was able to beat, via decision, a very physical looking twenty-five year old man. I weighed only 150 lbs at the time.

My grandfather owned a large dairy farm in White Creek, New York, and he would encourage me and Dan to continue boxing. Whenever I fought locally either in Bennington, Hoosick Falls or the Petersburg area, he and a group of his friends were always in attendance. I spent a lot of time with my grandfather weekends, during school and summer vacations.

He would tell me that when he was in school, kids would box during school recess, and when he was a bit older, young men would fight in the street right outside the hotel in Eagle Bridge, New York. Not sanctioned bouts, of course, but just for fun.

I started keeping two pairs of boxing gloves in my grandfathers car and would box people wherever we would go. My cousins, people who worked on my grandfather's farm, anyone, anywhere. The people I would box against were usually bigger and older than me.

Hoosick Falls, New York, is very close to Bennington, and many of the kids in the boxing club were from Bennington. With a lot of club members from Vermont, the Vermont Golden Gloves was a really big event. If you won, that meant you were THE CHAMP!

Vermont Golden Gloves Experience

The first year I entered the Vermont Golden Gloves in 1985, I had only one bout under my belt. At that time there was no novice division [eight bouts or less], as it was an open class tournament which meant the opponent you faced could have an unlimited number of bouts. I was only sixteen years old and entering the gloves was an eye opening experience. Being held since the mid-1940s at Burlington Memorial Auditorium, the place was huge. There were boxers milling around, weigh-ins and registrations going on. For those who have never been to Memorial Auditorium, there are bleachers on each side, ringside and balcony seating. The ring, of course, is set up in the middle of the floor, which is a full sized basketball court. When boxing begins, the lights are turned down except for the ring light, which is lowered from the ceiling. It really gives you the air and atmosphere of boxing in a professional event. I loved it! I have boxed in a number of places and events over the years, but none are run better than the Vermont Golden Gloves. The only other event that draws a bigger crowd is the New England Golden Gloves Tournament of Champions in Lowell, Massachusetts. The Lowell auditorium is much bigger and if Burlington Memorial was larger I'm sure there would be more in attendance as well.

Luckily, I was matched with another inexperienced boxer for my first golden gloves match. I beat Joe-Joe Malzac in the quarter-finals of the 147 lb class when he didn't come out of his corner for the second round. The Vermont Golden Gloves is run for three consecutive Saturday nights, so I only had a week to celebrate my victory. My next match, in the semi-finals, wasn't so easy. I lost a very close decision to Bill Spurr, a twenty-two year old Middlebury College student who was a Washington state native with over one hundred amateur fights. Not bad for a sixteen year old who had only two previous matches.

In 1986, I moved up a weight class to 156 and beat Dale Pearson, of the Oakley Boxing Club out of Claremont, New Hampshire, on opening night. I was actually nervous about boxing Dale as I knew he had more experience than me. Dale had actually fought a couple of the boxers from the Hoosick Club, boxers that I knew. Even though the Hoosick Falls boxers had won, I was still leery about boxing Dale. I boxed very well and won the match. The next week in the semi's I had to box twice in one night [that was allowed in those days]. First I boxed George Dovas whom I beat on a third round TKO. Of course, I didn't have to box the two matches one right after the other. I fought the first match of the night and the second one was at the end of the nights card. In the finals that year, I lost a close decision to Shon Marcotte. Marcotte was out of the Lyn-J Boxing Club and his trainer/coach was Victor Gammell, who was Chief of Officials in Vermont. Shon probably had the most potential of any boxer I ever fought and was probably the best fighter I ever did fight. He could punch as hard as a horse kicks, was lightning quick, very strong, could take a tremendous punch–had a granite jaw–excellent boxing skills, and was naturally in good condition. Even though I lost the match, I was very happy, as no one thought I would go the distance against Marcotte. This was my very best fight to this point. I was also voted the Outstanding Sportsman of the 1986 Vermont Golden Gloves. The trophy is one of the biggest and nicest ones I have.

I entered the Vermont Golden Gloves in 1987 at 156 lbs eager for a rematch with Shon Marcotte, instead I lost by decision on the opening night to Tim Burrows of Maine. Burrows went on to defeat Shon by decision in the finals. He was not only the 156 lb champion, but was also voted the Outstanding Boxer of the tournament. This was the third year in a row that I had failed to win this tournament.

Better Sparring and More Ring Time

In addition to going to the Hoosick Falls Club I also went to the Uncle Sam Boxing Club in Troy and the South Mall Boxing Club in Albany, New York. At both of these clubs I had the opportunity to spar with professional boxers. Bob Miller, who owned and operated Uncle Sams would take me along with his boxing team and got me a lot of bouts against some very good boxers. Bob was always traveling to different venues with his team, not only in the United States but also in Canada.

In Ontario, Canada, I beat the undefeated Ontario light heavyweight champion. At the Empire State Games in Syracuse, New York, I won a bronze medal, getting byed all the way into the medal round. Then I got beat by the eventual gold medalist. The boxing was held in the Carrier Dome with a seating capacity of 66,000. There were other events going on as well during the Empire Games, and there were probably two hundred spectators in the Dome a small crowd for such a large place. I also boxed in the New York Gloves as well as at the New York State Fairgrounds, both in Syracuse.

Now I'm ready to win the Gloves!

After gaining much experience sparring pros and boxing high quality fighters, I was ready to win the Vermont Golden Gloves. I went back in 1988 at 165 lbs and never lost another Vermont Golden Gloves match. On the opening night in 1988, I beat Ray Boom Boom Piquette by a second round TKO. He was the runner-up the year before. I got a bye in the semi's and beat Scott Shaddock of Rutland in the finals by a second round TKO. I didn't enter the gloves in 1989 due to an injury while in training. However, in 1990, I was back at 178 lbs, probably my best weight to box at. In the semi-finals I defeated Brian Mosher by a second round TKO, and in the finals I beat Jason Leo in a first round TKO.

My next stop was the New England Golden Gloves Tournament of Champions in Lowell, Massachusetts. It's two nights of boxing involving four teams, Lowell Sun, Holyoke Boys Club, Southern New England and Vermont. Holyoke has since been replaced with a team from Connecticut. This is a very tough tournament to win, as there are many talented boxers who participate plus you have a home town team, the Lowell Sun to contend with.

Still Talking About My New England Championship Match

The first night in Lowell, in 1990, which would be the semi-finals, I boxed Joe Machon from Holyoke and won a three round decision. The second night, for the New England Championship I boxed Roberto Vasquez of Lowell, and again won a three round decision. This was a very tough win for me as it was a wild slugfest for all three rounds. What a match! This was the type of fight so action packed, that it stuck in many fans minds for years. In fact, ten years after that bout, people were still talking about it as far away as Las Vegas.

Back to the Vermont Tournament

In 1991, I dropped weight and went back to the Vermont Golden Gloves at 165 lbs. On opening night I beat Chris Shaddock, brother of Scott Shaddock whom I had beaten in 1988. I beat Chris in a three round decision. He had an awkward style and I expected a slugfest, but he threw me off by attempting to box me. He actually frustrated me during the whole bout. In the semi-finals, I beat Charles Roderick, Jr., by a first round TKO. I felt sorry for Roderick as he had already boxed once that night before boxing me. In the finals, I beat Josh Mason by a first round TKO.

In Lowell that year, I beat Devon Clark in the semi-finals on a three round decision. He was tough. I knocked him down once but he got off the canvas and kept on fighting. I badly injured my left hand in that bout and should have withdrawn from the tournament, but instead I wanted to give it my best shot. In the championship match with Dan Constantino, I could not properly defend myself, and though I did manage to stagger and stun Constantino causing him to get a standing eight count, the ref stopped the match with thirty seconds left in the first round.

In 1992, I went back to the Vermont Golden Gloves at 165 lbs and got a bye all the way into the finals, as there were only two other entries in that class. Those two boxers, from the same club, fought each other on opening night. Erwin Moritz won the match on a decision. Erwin had a lot of heart in the finals, and gave a really good effort. He was trained by Jimmy Sheridan, one of the best trainers at the Vermont Golden Gloves. I beat Moritz on a second round TKO. In addition to winning the championship, I was also voted the 1992 Vermont Golden Gloves Outstanding Boxer. That was an honor with a nice trophy to go along with it.

Now it was off to Lowell and the New Englands where I was beaten on opening night by Jose Anaiaga. I had to lose too much weight at the time to make the 165 lb class. I made the weight in Vermont but was way too weak, dehydrated and sluggish to win that year in Lowell, I weighed in right beside John Ruiz who later became World Heavyweight Champion. He was only one weight class above me at the time.

I'll back track a little and write about how I did in the New Englands the first time I was there in 1988 at 165 lbs. I boxed a guy named John Scully, he was the #3 ranked amateur middleweight in the USA at the time. John used to spar Marvin Haglers half brother, Robbie Simms who beat Roberto Duran once, and also fought for the middleweight championship. The reports that we were getting from people all said that Scully used to beat Simms easily. When I fought Scully I had nowhere near enough experience to compete with him. The ref and my coach Don Hamilton both decided to stop the match after the first round. I have remained friends with John Scully to this day, and we correspond on a regular basis.

Remembering Bernie Cummings

Once in Lowell, at the New England Golden Gloves in 1990 the year I had defeated Joe Machon, Bernie and Ernie Farrar were in my motel room along with my coach Don Hamilton. Bernie asked Don if it was OK to show me something. Don agreed, and Bernie begins to demonstrate how he thought I should fight Roberto Vasquez. Bernie had lots of boxing knowledge as he had been a professional boxer himself. I really appreciated him encouraging me and showing me things to help me win.

It really makes me feel good when I go back to the Vermont Golden Gloves and people recognize me, say hello and call me by name and shake my hand. One year there were several pictures of myself in the Vermont Golden Gloves program book. I had been retired from boxing since 2001, yet the fans still recognized me and asked me to autograph the program books they had. That makes you feel important!

1996
Reflections On My Brother
by Jeff Batchelder

Dan Batchelder

My brother Dan was six when he started going to the gym. There were about twenty kids at the Hoosick Falls Boxing Club with all different styles, and Dan would spar with them all. He was also fighting a lot of Junior Olympic matches and really got quite good. When I stopped boxing in 1992, I would take Dan around to the gyms I had gone to in Troy, Albany and Saratoga, New York. The people there knew that Dan was worth investing time with, so he got a lot of first class training. I would also take Dan up to Hampton, New York, to spar with Tom Panouchek. I once boxed Tom in a five round bout in the old Rutland High School. I won, but it was a tough bout. Tom Panouchek vs Paul Reis in 1989 was one of the best Vermont Golden Gloves matches I ever saw.

Dan won the Vermont Golden Gloves three times between 1993 and 1996. In 1994, Dan lost a decision to Kenny Bouchard of Maine, but the next year he trained seriously and KOd Bouchard in the second round. He was voted the Vermont Golden Gloves Tournament Outstanding Boxer [Open Class] in both 1993 and 1995. Dan's Vermont Golden Gloves Tournament record stands at nine wins [six by TKO], one loss, and three Championships, 1993, 1995 and 1996 [all open class].

Dan won the New England Golden Gloves in 1996 as a light heavy-weight at 178 lbs. He went on to the Nationals that year along with Domingo Macho Laboy–a 147 lb boxer from Troy, New York, who had also won the Vermont Golden Gloves that year. Dan made it all the way to the semi-finals at the Nationals.

Soon after losing in the semi-final round at the Nationals Dan turned professional. He was originally trained out of Albany, New York, but then went on to the Mike Tyson camp, and eventually to Arizona. Dan started boxing professionally in the super middleweight class at 168 lbs., and was ranked as high as #7 in the world by the World Boxing Council. He also boxed at 175 lbs and moved to cruiserweight at 200 lbs, where he was consistently ranked #9 or #10 in the world by the WBC. Dan is currently boxing as a heavyweight and weighs in at 220-225 lbs.

Dan has been ranked as high as #7 in the world as a professional boxer by the WBC. He won the World Boxing Association–Fedalatin Light Heavyweight Title, the North American Boxing Council Cruiserweight Title, and the WBC Continental Americas Cruiserweight Title as well.

Victor Gammell
"They Know Who I Am"

Victor Gammell (center).

Many years ago before Victor had any thought or idea about becoming a USA Boxing official, he traveled throughout New England and Canada. No, not sight seeing but as a coach/trainer with his team of boxers from the Lyn-J Boxing Club based out of St. Johnsbury,Vermont. Boxing aficionado, Victor Gammell, had the idea of starting a boxing club, giving youngsters, something to do besides roaming the streets or sitting in front of a television. Word got around the Lyndonville/St. Johnsbury area that a boxing club was being organized and it wasn't long before he had a group of prospective boxers. Finding a training site has always been difficult but the club did find space to train at the St. Johnsbury recreation center. In fact, it was in the rec center that Victor put on a club show and, eventual, four time Vermont and New England heavy-weight champion Tony Robitaille had one of his first bouts, if not his first.

Victor trained many boxers in his day and two of them come to mind at this time. Shon Marcotte and Joe Allard. Shon started training when he was about 8 years old and went on to win the Vermont Golden Gloves Championship twice once at 147 lbs and again at 156 lbs. Shon started boxing long before the USA Boxing Junior division was ever thought of and never boxed in the novice division. He would box anyone and everyone from the time he stepped into the ring for the first time all through the years until he retired. Today, a boxer or a coach wants to know how many matches their opponent has, what's their record, how tall is he, what kind of boxer is he, etc. Victor knew that Shon could be matched up with most anyone in his weight class. He was trained properly and had the ring savvy and expertise to box anyone, and the proper attitude that you had to box "all comers" to get to the top and never asked questions. He boxed in Montreal and throughout New England, against some very tough opponents, many times, and won. Shon was the hardest puncher in his weight class. Former Golden Gloves Champion Jeffrey Batchelder out of Schuylerville, New York, can attest to that. In my conversations with Jeff, he will always bring up the fact that Shon Marcotte was the hardest puncher he ever faced, besides being a nice guy and one heck of a boxer. Shon was the best.

Joe Allard was another boxer out of the same mold as Shon. A prolific puncher and boxer. He would travel the length of the state and throughout New England and Canada to box. Joe would also box anyone in his 178 lb weight class as he had the attitude that you had to box anyone and everyone to get to the top. Jim Churchill, one of the best boxers to come out of the state of Vermont, defeated Joe one year in the Vermont Golden Gloves for the championship. Jim told me recently, "My match with Joe was action packed, he was tough but a very decent man. He's the type of guy that could be anyone's best friend." Joe is following in the footsteps of his former mentor and has started his own boxing club in West Burke, Vermont. His son Anthony, won the 2007 Vermont Golden Gloves Novice Championship. Victor spent numerous hours with his boxers and instilled a lot of pride in them. Not only were they good sportsmen in the ring but outside the ropes as well.

As boxers get older, things do change. Joe joined the U.S. Coast Guard and Shon went on to the business world. As things slowed down, Victor headed to the warmer climate of Florida. After a few years of working in the hot sun, it was time to come back to the cooler climate of the Green Mountain State. Instead of training boxers and starting another club, Victor decided he wanted to become an official. He would referee or judge a bout wherever he was needed. Today, he is one of the top referees in New England. Not only does he officiate in Vermont but throughout New England and New York as well. Victor is now refereeing in the pro ranks, as well as the amateurs, and has been seen on ESPN's "Friday Night Fights". Victor will leave at a moments notice and head to a boxing match when the New England/USA Boxing Chief of Officials, Ray Delicio gives him a call and tell him he's needed. Distance doesn't matter to him. It's because of his knowledge and dedication to the sport that Ray appointed Victor Chief of Officials for the state of Vermont in 2005. As Chief of officials, Victor appoints and oversees all officials at a boxing event whether it's a club show or an advancing tournament. I have known Victor for many years as a truly dedicated individual to the sport of boxing from the time he was a coach/trainer, a judge, a referee and now Chief of Officials. He has always been the type of person who is willing to lend a helping hand whenever and wherever it's needed.

Even though Victor has put many hours into training boxers or officiating at many amateur and professional boxing venues, over the years, he was never alone, he has always had the support of his family. His three daughters, Sarah, Tonya and Sadie can usually be found wherever their father is officiating a boxing match, whether in Vermont or elsewhere in New England. Sadie followed in her fathers foot steps and became a certified USA Boxing official. She judged many events, and worked her way up the ladder to clerking shows as well as being the USA Boxing/New England registration person for Vermont for a few years. Raising a family and the working world has taken Sadie out of boxing for awhile, however, she is always there supporting her father.

"They Know Who I Am" was the headline on the sports page of the Lowell Sun newspaper. Victor had refereed, the night before, a match in the New England Golden Gloves Tournament of Champions. The next afternoon he rushed into my room all excited asking if I had seen the newspaper. Thinking something drastic had happened, told him I hadn't read the paper today. That's when he showed me the paper. It was a picture of him refereeing a match with that memorable headline. We have had a lot of fun with Victor and that headline. After all, it was the first time he had refereed in the Lowell tournament, and already they knew who Victor Gammell was! Actually, the story beneath that headline was about many times New England Golden Gloves Champion Edwin Rodriguez, who went on to win a National Championship. They knew who he was in Lowell!

Victor resides in St. Johnsbury and is employed in the Maintenance Department of Northern Community Management Company. When not working or officiating a boxing match, he usually heads for the wilderness. He's an outdoorsman and an excellent hunter and has bagged many deer along with a moose. When Victor bags the largest deer or moose in the state, the headline in many newspapers will read, "They Know Who I Am!!!"

Victor Gammell (left-holding bag) and Shon Marcotte (right). August 23, 1984.

1988
Bob Dragon
Burlington's Heavyweight Champion

Bobby started boxing in the Vermont Golden Gloves in 1982 when he was 17 years old, starting out in the 147 lb class and progressing right up to the heavyweight class. Along the way it seemed he was always in the finals but could never quite capture the big win until 1988. That year Bobby was just slightly over the light heavyweight limit, and so he had to enter the gloves in the heavyweight division. He won both preliminary matches and had to box tough Angelo Iachetta of Rutland for the championship. Angelo, who had won the 1986 championship, weighed in at 250 pounds! Iacheeta's trainer, Tommy Garrow, remarked at the time– "When Dragon comes to fight, you really have to box to beat him because he's a tough kid." Slugging isn't a smart way to go against Dragon. It should be an interesting fight though, I can't wait to see it." It was indeed an interesting and exciting fight that brought the house down! For three fast and furious rounds they mixed it up. Bob being smaller and nearly 50 pounds lighter than Angelo was the quicker of the two, but Angelo got his punches in as well. In the end, the decision went to Bob.

Bob Dragon was more than a boxer–deep down he was a kind hearted individual willing to help almost anyone. It was Bob and Joe Stone, another golden gloves boxer, who helped train Duxbury's Scott Patterson, who went on to win numerous state championships. Scott traveled to the Burlington Boys' Club to train with Bob and Joe until his father, Ed built a gym in a barn at their home.

Bob was an avid sports fan, whether it was boxing, hunting, fishing, basketball, football or auto racing. Bob raced cars at Barre's Thunder Road and Plattsburgh's Airborne Speedway. He was as aggressive on the oval as he was in the ring, and in racing circles he was known as "The Burlington Bad Boy!"

Bob also helped organize a fundraiser or "smoker" or club bout for the Union 32 High School athletic boosters club, helped organize several basketball leagues, coached on the youth level, and umpired many Little League baseball games around the Burlington area.

Bob boxed many tough opponents in his career–one of them being "Sugar" Ray Daniels of Glens Falls, New York, who defeated him for the 1986 championship on a decision. Daniels went on to win the New England Golden Gloves Championship. When Bob won the heavyweight championship in 1988, he went to Lowell, Massachusetts, where he lost a decision in the semi-finals to three-time heavyweight champion James Johnson. Bob had a very impressive record with 23 wins and 11 losses.

Bob took a hiatus from boxing for a few years, but then got the "itch" to return to the ring and the Vermont Golden Gloves Tournament in January. 2000, but was disqualified for being "too old"–thirty-four being the age limit at the time.

Unfortunately, Robert D. Dragon passed away unexpectedly on January 22, 2005. The Vermont Golden Gloves now includes a Senior Division for thirty-five year olds-plus in the tournament. So you see, Bob, really, you're never too old to step into the ring!

Portland's Bobby Russo:
A Trainer of Champions

Bobby Russo (right). Colorado Springs, Colorado, June, 2007. Lisa Kuronya (left), Defending National Champion and Captain of the USA Boxing Team, wins her second consecutive USA title.

George Russo, a former Maine Boxing Commissioner and Bobby's uncle, introduced him to boxing before he was ten years old. He would take Bobby to the weekly boxing matches at the Portland Expo, which was a hot bed of boxing in the 1960s and 1970s. A young Bobby started training and sparring at the Arena gym when he was twelve, but never boxed competitively because of poor eye sight. Bobby loved the sport though and was always hanging around the gym.

In his late teens, Bobby traveled to Las Vegas to find work. There were plenty of gyms for him to hang out in, but it was at Johnny Garcia's Main Street Gym that he would meet hall of fame trainer Chuck Bodak. There were plenty of world class boxers who would show up at the gym–the likes of Sugar Ray Leonard, Roberto Duran, and Tommy Hearns to name a few. Bodak was a wealth of knowledge and a great "basics" coach, Bobby recalled. "He was all about balance–it was a great education." That experience would eventually transfer to his Portland Boxing Club. It's the reason Bobby's boxers always look good–grounded in the basics and good balance.

Bobby's stint out west shaped his coaching and training style, which has led to great things for his Portland Boxing Club. Arriving back in Maine, a friend approached Bobby who had a relative who wanted to box, and Bobby agreed to train him. There soon came along more prospective boxers to train and coach, such as Jessie DiBiase–who would go on to win a Golden Glove title. It wasn't long before the Portland Boxing Club was organized.

The Portland Boxing Club has come a long way since then, with great success. Bobby and his club can boast of over 100 championships, as well as boxers who have participated in the Olympic trials, a reigning women's World Amateur Welterweight Champion, a Bronze medalist in the Pan-Am Championships, two U. S. Boxing National Golden Gloves Champions–plus an undefeated welterweight pro, Jason LeHoullier. In brief–Bobby has a gym full of champions!

Bobby created and directs the Northeastern Regional Boxing Championships–a very popular event–held each year in the fall in Portland, Maine. He also takes his team to Oregon for a Portland versus Portland event. He certainly doesn't sit on his laurels that's for sure. Bobby is always on the move with his club.

There's always a long waiting list to join the Portland Boxing Club, and if a newcomer thinks that he or she can immediately get into the ring and start sparring–think again! Bobby will have that newcomer working with the veterans until they prove both their talent and dedication. It takes at least three months to learn the basics before any sparring takes place.

Bobby has been entering boxers in the Vermont Golden Gloves tournament since he started his club. A very courteous group of young men and women–when they get into the ring it's all business! Through the years Portland has had many Vermont and New England Golden Gloves champions. When asked why Portland boxers have been so successful over the years, Bobby says–"It's all about the "basics.""

2000
Jason "The Hammer" LeHoullier
From Vermont Golden Gloves to ESPN's Friday Night Fights

Jason LeHoullier

When Jason walked into the Portland Boxing Club in 1997, and asked Bobby Russo to be his trainer, little did he know that he would be making boxing history. Jason had dropped out of Dover High School in New

Hampshire, and as a troubled teenager without direction, was losing in street fights. With little ring experience, Bobby Russo took this young man of raw talent, and molded him into a professional boxer with an impressive 20 plus professional wins to his credit. Along the way, Jason compiled an amateur record of 40 wins and 10 losses. In 2000, he won the Vermont Golden Gloves at 147 lbs, defeating Chris Lane currently of Seacoast Boxing in Rochester, New Hampshire. He went on to win the New England Golden Gloves Tournament of Champions in Lowell, Massachusetts, and then on to the National Golden Gloves in Detroit, where he won his first match.

Jason moved up in weight to the 156 lbs class and won the 2001 Vermont Golden Gloves, defeating Josie Grandbois out of Jim Sheridan's Tri-Town Boxing Club. He also won the USA New England Boxing tournament and boxed in the Eastern Olympic Trials. Jason won the Northeast Regional Tournament, held in Portland, Maine, so many times that nobody wanted to box him. The "Hammer" was one tough skilled boxer!

In amateur boxing you can reach a point where you become known as an excellent boxer and puncher, that it becomes impossible to find matches. That's what happened to Jason. "I reached the point in amateurs where I couldn't go much further, and it was either move into the pro ranks or retire," Jason remembers. "My style was more conducive to professional boxing–I'm a body puncher. Amateurs are about scoring points–pros are about KOs," he added.

Jason "The Hammer" LeHoullier made his pro, in a scheduled four rounder, on July 13, 2001, at the Hampton Beach Casino in New Hampshire. He boxed Miguel Colon and scored a TKO in round three. Since then, Jason has been seen frequently on ESPN Television's Friday Night Fights.

"My amateur career was full of great memories, new experiences, and it took me places I never thought I'd go, and did things I never thought I'd do. I started boxing late, but found my competitive spirit once again. Through the guidance and support of great people I met through boxing and coaching, I realized the only thing holding me back was me. Anything is possible," said LeHoullier as he reflected on the past.

Jason came a long way since dropping out of high school, and getting into street fights. It can truly be said that boxing changed his life. While attending college in Maine, Jason "The Hammer" keeps on punching!

2002
Joey Lefebvre: Vermont's First New England Golden Gloves Novice Champion

Joey Lefebvre, New England Golden Gloves Champion, 2002.

In 2002, the Lowell Sun newspaper, the New England Golden Gloves franchise holder, instituted the New England wide novice tournament. That meant novice champions from Vermont, Southern New England, Connecticut and Lowell, Massachusetts–all franchise holders under the Lowell sun–could now advance to the "big" tournament. In the past, novices did not advance past their respective tournaments.

That year, Joey Lefebvre of Bantam Boxing Club in Winooski, entered the Vermont Golden Gloves Tournament. He got a "bye" in the first round, but then made short work in the semi's and finals scoring TKO's in both matches. In his semi-final match, he faced Ryan Gagner of Rampage Boxing Club. Lefebvre came out dancing around his opponent in the defensive mode, then toward the end of the first came on with a flurry of punches to win by TKO when Gagner retired. Joey scored another TKO in the finals defeating a young boxer by the name of Jonathan Mears. With the Vermont tournament behind him, and with a championship in hand, it was time to head to Lowell, Massachusetts, and the New England Golden Gloves Novice Tournament of Champions.

In the semi-finals, Joey drew Omar Medina out of the Southern New England Golden Gloves Tournament. Young Lefebvre picked up where he left off in Vermont. According to the Lowell Sun, for the better part of two plus rounds neither boxer held anything back–it was a "pier six" brawl. sooner or later something had to give, and it turned out to be Joey's legs as he dropped to a knee after being rattled by a wicked volley of shots.

Instead of heading to a neutral corner, Medina of Fall River, pressed for the KO. Before referee Nick Previtti could step in and give an eight count, Medina tagged Joey with several shots to the head and body. Previtti immediately disqualified Medina and awarded the victory, forty-six seconds into the third round, to nineteen year old, Joey Lefebvre of Underhill.

Nick Previtti, a long time Golden Gloves referee knew that he did the right thing by stopping the fight–with Nick safety came first. Neither Medina or his cornerman protested the ruling. In the dressing room after the bout, the eighteen year old Medina, who had won the Southern New England Tournament by a "walkover" and was making his amateur debut, was just glad Lefebvre wasn't hurt. Joey, a member of the Vermont National Guard, was on standby status at the time of the tournament and was called to duty soon after and served a tour in Iraq.

At 125 lbs Joey, trained and coached by his dad Billy, was now ready to win the New England Championship. Joey is a third generation Golden Gloves Boxer–his grandfather Bobby, and his father are both former champions, and he wanted to continue that tradition. That he did when he defeated Shaun Hildreth, a Lowell boxer, in the finals for the New England Golden Gloves Novice Championship.

"Blood, Sweat–But No Tears–Lefebvre and Hildreth Went to War!"

In the next newly released edition of Websters Dictionary, if you look up the word "Battle" you will find its definition and a photo of Shaun Hildreth and Joe Lefebvre! Seriously, you don't see many fights like this at the novice division. In the first round of this fight, Hildreth got off to a good start by attacking Lefebvre and scoring with nice jabs and combinations. About mid way through Lefebvre lands a solid right hand right on the nose of Hildreth and the blood was gushing. In between rounds, West End Gym cornerman, Joey Ramalho, could only apply pressure and hoped the bleeding would stop and not hamper the breathing of his charge. The bleeding did stop but not for long. One stiff jab from Lefebvre opens the floodgates again and Hildreth is a mess. Nevertheless, Hildreth presses forward and its all out war between these two. It was non-stop punching by both warriors and while the battle was on the ropes, us folks at ringside got a bit of a red paint-job as the blood flew with every punch. Although Hildreth looked the worse for ware, the second round was a good one for him. Lefebvre may have sense that he came up a bit short in the second and came out winging in round three. Toe to toe, punch for punch they swapped blows. With just 15 seconds remaining in the fight, Lefebvre lands a perfect right hand that sends Hildreth down. That one punch may have been the telling point that sealed it for Lefebvre. Hildreth was back on his feet and allowed to continue but there was no time left. This was a great fight and it's a shame that either had to lose but one always does in amateur boxing. Joe Lefebvre gets the nod from the judges and becomes the 125-pound New England Novice Champion. Good fight guys, I'll send you my dry-cleaning bill!!!!

"Thanks to Jerry Colton and his article."

James A. "Benjy" Bonilla
In Memory
Vermont Golden Gloves "Sportsmanship Award"

James A. "Benjy" Bonilla

Amateur boxing, and in particular the Vermont Golden Gloves, lost a very close friend with the passing of James A. "Benjy" Bonilla in 2006. Benjy, from Rutland, was a fixture at the "gloves" as he was a certified official with USA Boxing, and could be seen at ringside as a judge, or even on the stage at the auditorium as a glover/inspector. He'd always asked–"What do you want me to do tonight boss?" Whatever was asked of him he'd always do a class "A" job. Benjy was the "go to guy" whenever you needed help, and a simple phone call to let him know where the boxing show was next, would have him saying–"I'll be there."

Benjy boxed in the Vermont Golden Gloves in the early 1980s when Tommy Garrow ran the Rutland Boxing Club. With Tommy at the helm you could always count on a very tough team of boxers, and Benjy was one of them. He boxed in the heavyweight class, at a time when super heavyweight had yet to be invented, and the "big guy" was always ready to box when he stepped into the ring.

Benjy graduated from Mount St. Joseph Academy and was president of the class of 1975. He was very community minded, and as a member of the Kiwanis Club of Rutland started the annual "bike rodeo" in that city. He was also on the advisory board of the Salvation Army, and helped start the "Stuff-A-Bus" with Capt. John Bennett. He also volunteered for the Knights of Columbus, and was an assistant coach for the 7/8th grade tackle football program. "Big Benjy B Promotions" did, indeed, promote just about anything and everything–including pro wrestling and professional boxing in the Rutland area.

Until his illness in 1990, he was a food salesman for Independent Food Company in Burlington. We'll all miss Benjy and the tales he told about the early days of boxing in Rutland.

"Fellowship of the Ring"–by Ken Picard
Armand Gelineau

First appeared in the January 28, 2004 issue of Seven Days
Edited by Bob Winkler

Armand Gelineau

The staccato beat of boxing gloves on a leather speed bag fills the air of the dilapidated old barroom on Wolcott Street in downtown Hardwick, home of the Hardwick Amateur Boxing Club. As the chickita chickita patter announces the start of another Tuesday night workout, Armand Gelineau, the club's 78 year-old trainer, paces impatiently and swears to himself. He's waiting for the rest of his young boxers to trickle in the door.

"They come and go like a bunch of sheep," Gelineau gripes, his thick Northeast Kingdom accent garbled by a mashed lower jaw, the result of countless bare-fisted blows he took in his youth. "There's five already gone to a basketball game, and four more right here in the village that haven't showed up and probably won't. So, it's hard getting 'em in."

Gelineau is short, with wiry salt-n-pepper hair, poor hearing, and dark eyes that dart about behind his thick black glasses. About fifteen guys and one girl have signed up for the Hardwick Amateur Boxing Club since Gelineau opened it in September 2002. They range in age from 14 to 30. The unsteady rhythm of the speed bag is a reminder that most of them haven't had much experience hitting anything that moves or hits back.

But if the boxers are new, nearly everything else in the gym is a holdover from a bygone era: the old brass ringside bell mounted on a loose piece of plywood, the antique boxing glove spray painted gold that someone mounted on a stick, the faded black and white poster advertising the "Cy Perkins' Boxing Show" at Community Hall in Montpelier. Reserved seats for that February 1942 event cost 90 cents, but soldiers and sailors could get in for a quarter.

Another fight card on the wall announces a bout featuring Burlington's Charlie "Buster" Beaupre, a lightweight state champion in the mid-1930s. Beaupre's cousin was a dentist who made Gelineau his first mouthpiece so he could go train in Boston, until Gelineau's mother got wind of the plan and forbid it.

Actually, nothing in the gym is as much of a holdover from Vermont's pugilistic past as Gelineau himself. Local boxing old timers describe him as "definitely old school," someone who "swears like a parrot" but has a heart bigger than a racehorses, or simply "a character."

Gelineau has spent much of his life pursuing his boyhood dream to own a gym, become a trainer and promote amateur bouts. And while no one in the boxing world describes his career as a success in the traditional sense–he's lost more money than he's made and never sent a boxer to a national championship– Gelineau has yet to throw in the towel. In fact, despite a hardscrabble history marked by heavy drinking, fighting and personal tragedies, Gelineau still devotes most of his time, energy and money to teaching young people in his working class community what he calls "the sweet science of boxing."

On a recent evening, Gelineau is readying three of his four boxers who are heading to the Burlington Golden Gloves. Among them is seventeen year old, Lori Martin, the club's only female and heavyweight. Martin, who used to get into frequent brawls in high school, says she switched to boxing after watching the Rocky movies. Though she has never fought competitively, she is dying to climb into the ring. "I try to get some of my girlfriends to come down so I can spar with them, but a lot of girls aren't really interested in boxing," Martin says.

Gelineau points out one of his more promising fighters, 26 year-old Brock Billings. The 163 pound propane technician from Walden, whose shaved head and "Mad Dog" tattoo complement an already intimidating stare, used to compete in kick boxing and Tae Kwon Do tournaments before joining the Hardwick club. When asked what kind of coach Gelineau is, he says, "hard to understand sometimes, but other than that, it's up to the individual if they want to work hard."

The third rookie in the tournament is 25 year-old Peter Hirschfeld, a cops-n-courts reporter for the Times-Argus–who is working on a first person account of training for the Golden Gloves. Hirschfeld, who's only been boxing with Gelineau for a couple of months, recalls how on his first day at the gym he met a boxer in his mid-twenties who never returned. Hirschfeld later found out the guy had been sent back to jail. Gelineau had bailed him out a couple of times, given him a blanket, and let him sleep in the gym until he was back on his feet.

Gelineau knows what it's like to be down for the count–both inside and outside of the ring. "I use to drink a lot. I spent twenty of my best years drinking," he admits. "So I says, look I don't want the kids to do what I done, lose the best part of their life. I'm gonna start a boxing club, a gym, so they can be straight. So I did."

When Gelineau tells a story, it's hard to know whether he's talking about last year or 1930–he shuffles back and forth in time a lot, like a prize fighter dancing around the canvas. He says he only stepped into the ring once as a boxer himself, and that was enough. It was years ago–Gelineau can't recall when–and the Hardwick Fire Department had sponsored a town fair that included a boxing match. His opponent, a big bruiser from New Hampshire, climbed into the ring weighting 50 pounds more than he did. "Oh, by God, boy!" exclaims Gelineau, looking back on the fight. "He threw a right hand and my head's still dizzy since then."

Which isn't to say that Gelineau never threw his share of punches outside the ring. He grew up on a farm in West Charleston and learned to box at age 14 from his older brothers. "Back then, we used to fight for jackknives and fish poles," he recalls. Then the Great Depression hit. The family farm went belly up and they had to abandon the place. "We left there with a one-horse buggy, three bags of potatoes and the clothes on our back," Gelineau recalled.

"I came to Hardwick in 1938, 'cause Hardwick was a fightin' town in the stone-shedding days," he continued. "There were fourteen barrooms in Hardwick and three restaurants. There was no suction device in the granite buildings in them days, so that dust–ah, Jesus!–plugged their lungs right up, so they'd only last 40 years and come down with the stonecutter consumption."

For men like Gelineau, who didn't get jobs in the granite sheds, money was hard to come by. Occasionally, he picked up a few days work building roads for the Civilian Conservation Corps, then supplemented his income at the Saturday night bouts, where spectators threw money right into the ring for the contenders. And with all the granite sheds, there were plenty of burly armed brawlers around looking to prove themselves.

The fights weren't exactly formal affairs. Gelineau remembered how the men used to gather in whatever space they could find–a barn, armory, schoolhouse, even a farmhouse kitchen–and slug it out for $5 or $10. "We used to move the chairs and tables out, round up a mess of boys and let'er go. No mouthpieces, no head-gear, no gloves, nothing! "We learned the art of fisticuffs, the sweet science of boxing, the hard way."

Since 1948 Vermont's Golden Gloves tournament has been held in Burlington's Memorial Auditorium, and amateur boxing saw a resurgence in the 1970s with the arrival of the U.S. Olympic team, which trained at the University of Vermont for the 1976 summer games in Montreal. That team included such legendary names as Sugar Ray Leonard, John Tate and Michael and Leon Spinks, all of whom went on to professional fame.

Of course, amateur boxing has never been about earning a living–after Michael Spinks won his gold medal that year, he quit the sport and went to work cleaning floors and scrubbing toilets in a St. Louis chemical factory. During the 1970, Gelineau also worked as a janitor in the Concord manufacturing plant in Morrisville while operating a boxing gym out of the old Hardwick fire station. After scraping together enough money to build a ring he could move from to town, Gelineau started sponsoring annual tournaments and "smoker matches" in places like St. Johnsbury, Newport, Morrisville and Hardwick. Invariably, those events lost money.

In 1979, Gelineau put on the Northeast Kingdom Tournament, which drew boxers from all over Vermont, Maine, New Hampshire and Massachusetts. He raffled off a ham to make some extra money while his wife sold cookies, donuts and coffee. The event cost him $6,000. He didn't fare well. "Lost my shirt," he admitted. The following year, he shaved $1,000 off the cost of the event but still ended up deep in the red. "I never got a dime. I was busted broke all the time. I spent $14,000 out of my own pocket to keep that boxing thing going for twelve years. There's no money in this gosh-damned business."

In the fall of 1980, Gelineau put on what would be his last tournament in Hardwick. It was a lean night and there weren't many sparring partners available. So when Shaun Moore, a 24-year old schoolteacher new to Hardwick's Hazen Union School, volunteered to spar with a young welterweight, Gelineau didn't think much of it. Both boxers were outfitted in head-gear, mouthpieces, athletic cups and 16-ounce gloves, and the canvas had the standard 3-inch pad.

When Moore took a single punch to the nose and collapsed in the sitting position, neither the referee nor the spectators suspected anything unusual had occurred. Three days later, he died of a concussion.

"If a boxing match is a story, it is always a wayward story, one in which anything can happen," writes Joyce Carol Oates, an avid boxing enthusiast. "In no other sport can so much take place in so brief a period of time, and so irrevocably."

About a week later, Gelineau returned from Moore's funeral in Holyoke, Massachusetts, locked the doors on his gym and had nothing to do with boxing for another two decades. These days, the usually talkative trainer doesn't offer may clues about how he spent those intervening years, except to say that he drank a lot.

Gelineau probably never would have returned to the sport if he didn't care much about young people. He began to notice a lot of Hardwick kids hanging around with nothing to do. "I see the kids running around the streets with their skateboards and their rollerblades and–oh, my God!– playing chicken in the road, futzing and farting and you name it! So I say, someone gonna get killed on this street so I better do something. So I started up the boxing club again."

Gelineau started visiting local businesses to raise money. He scraped together $5,500 in three weeks and bought new boxing gloves, protective gear and a new ring, which he set up in the local teen center. But a dispute would cost him his space and equipment. For a time, he tried to hold some matches in the rectory of St. Norbert's Church, but that didn't work out either. Eventually he told the priest, "Boxing and being in the church business don't go together too good."

Undaunted, Gelineau started again from scratch, visiting more businesses and scraping together another $1,200 so he could buy a ring and rent out the long defunct hotel on Wolcott Street. Like the old trainer, the hotel seems frozen in time–in the adjoining barroom, where the ceiling sags, there are still glasses on the bar and cigarettes in the ashtrays.

It's a struggle to make the gym work. With a modest Social Security check, supplemented by a part-time job as church custodian, Gelineau can barely afford the cost of heating the leaky old place. But he doesn't charge his club members more than $25 a month for their 3 hours sessions twice a week. "That's 24 hours of training for $25 bucks. And I have a hard time getting that. What I get, I get," Gelineau says with a shrug. "But I'm going to keep it open. Even if there's one or two of them, they'll learn something."

It's Saturday night in Memorial Auditorium for the first of three weekends of the Burlington Golden Gloves tournament. Downstairs, the locker room is a buzz with beefy-armed boys, a few of whom look like they've had their noses broken more than once, but there are plenty of nervous faces, too, including the Hardwick club's Dan "Bear" Bovat, a 172 pound middle-weight newcomer who's built like a fireplug. Bovat, whose grandfather was a Golden Gloves Champion, hops around anxiously trying to shake off his nervous energy. "I just want to get in there, fight, and get it over with," says Bovat, sipping water and spitting repeatedly into a trash can. He's vomited four times already, he admits, not to make weight but because of butterflies.

Gelineau and teammate Lori Martin wrap Bovat's hands while Gelineau gives him a last minute talk. Later that night there wasn't much to protect Bovat from the blows he takes from Newport's Todd Tewksbury. During the three-round bout, Bovat delivers a number of slow but solid punches of his own, but late in the second round he gets pinned in a corner, and has trouble getting out. He's still somewhat dazed as the third round begins, and the ref finally calls the fight in favor of Tewksbury. As Bovat spits out his mouth-piece and climbs dejectedly through the ropes, the spectator beside me comments, "That kid's got a lot of heart."

Hardwick's Brock Billings fares better. Just thirty seconds into the first round, he delivers a devastating uppercut to the Bantam Boxing Club's Matt

Huntington, sending his opponent to the canvas face down with one of the night's best thrown punches. Huntington survives the rest of the match, but the judges hand Billings a victory.

Hardwick's most surprising showing that night, however, is Peter Hirschfeld's three rounds against Green Mountain's Jeremy Bissonnett. From the opening bell, it's clear that neither fighter has set foot in the ring before–the fight is anything but graceful. By round two, Bissonnett is bleeding from the nose and both boxers are literally staggering with exhaustion. At the final bell, the contenders hug in a gesture of mutual respect. And when the announcer declares Bissonnett the winner by decision, the crowd lets out a chorus of sustained boos.

Back in the locker room Hirschfeld is just beginning to sense what he's going to feel like in the morning. Smiling weakly, the former sports writer expresses his unabashed relief that he won't be back next week to compete. "I don't want to bust on the Golden Gloves at all," Hirschfeld says–"but I don't ever want to do that again."

While Hirschfeld jokes about his impending punch hangover, two EMTs from the Burlington Fire Department are giving Bovat a thorough once-over. Apparently, he's still feeling dizzy and Gelineau isn't taking any chances.

Chapter Four

Women Pugilist

1994
Patty Lynch
"Boxing is so much more a mental sport of strategy to me."

Patty Lynch punches at sparring pads held by her trainer, Troy Tsounis. (Photo by Sandy Macys.)

Banners were waving throughout the crowd, "Go Patty!"–"Go Liza!" It was a packed Memorial Auditorium with the Championships of the Vermont Golden Gloves. Fans jammed the stands to witness the first ever sanctioned women's boxing match in the state of Vermont, thanks to the 1993 Federal Court ruling that declared the U.S. Amateur Boxing Federation's ban on female fighters unconstitutional. Women were now allowed to compete in the tournament for the first time. The fans didn't know what to expect. Would it be a brawl or boxing match. It was the latter!

Patty Lynch–singer, model, bartender, and waitress–was now Vermont's first female Golden Gloves Champion. In 1985, Patty moved from Texas to Vermont to be near her mother. She loved singing and soon joined "Little Wing"–a Burlington rock band as lead singer. She toured with them for four years, opening for such popular groups as "Deep Purple" and "Blue Oyster Cult." When "Little Wing" cut back it's schedule, Patty unable to survive on a part-time salary, took jobs waitressing and bartending. But she also had the urge to do something different with her life, and took up kickboxing at Moriarty's School of Kickboxing in Winooski.

In 1993, a young lady named Dallas Malloy had won the first ever female sanctioned boxing bout. I heard about that event, and so did my friend Paul Goldman of WVMT and 95 Triple X radio stations," Patty recalled. Paul encouraged Patty to enter the Vermont Golden Gloves, knowing that it would open up the sport in Vermont and New England. At the same time Patty entered the Vermont Golden Gloves tournament, Liza Walden (a University of Vermont student) also training at Moriarty's, entered the "gloves" to become Patty's opponent.

Both women trained separately under the watchful eyes of trainers Pete Ryan and Troy Tsounis–though they would spar each other on a weekly basis. Patty said the Liza was a very aggressive sparring partner, but knowing that she was going to be her opponent in the ring, didn't show here every trick she had up her sleeve. So she played the mental game with Liza. Boxing, Patty recalls, "Is so much more a mental sport of strategy to me, and that was always the most intriguing part for me. It's so much a physical chess game."

The Lynch/Walden bout was fantastic! It was a real boxing match with both boxers going toe-to-toe for most of the three rounds. It was history in the making with Patty Lynch winning the decision, and becoming the first ever female Vermont Golden Gloves Champion. Unfortunately, there were no women boxers entering the New England Golden Gloves in 1994, so Patty was unable to compete on a regional level.

In the 1995 Vermont Golden Gloves, Patty defeated Jill Cummings, a member of the Tri-Town Boxing Club out of Enosburg. Jill eventually left boxing and won the Miss Vermont title, and went on to Atlantic City and competed in the Miss American contest.

Patty had her first and only professional fight in 1997/98. The fight was scheduled for three rounds, and Patty outscored her opponent for the first two rounds. In the third round she caught a left hook to the temple, and although it only shook her up for a second or two, the referee stopped the fight awarding the victory to her opponent. "I was fine and had the advantage over my opponent, but the ref saw it differently," Patty recalled.

It was a short but very interesting boxing career for Patty Lynch–Vermont's first female Golden Gloves Champion. Patty currently lives in Arizona–and yes, she's still singing!

Portland's Lisa Kuronya–#1 in the USA

Lightweight Liz Leddy (left), and Welterweight Lisa Kuronya (right), both of the Portland Boxing Club, advance to the National Golden Gloves in Hollywood, Florida, July, 2007. Leddy advanced to the finals, but lost to the Number 1 ranked lightweight. Defending Golden Gloves Champion, Lisa Kuronya, won in the finals adding to her fourth National title. Leddy is ranked number 5 in the country and Kuronya is ranked number 1. Bobby Russo (center).

Lisa started boxing at the age of twenty-six to get into shape. However, in a short time under the influence of trainer Bobby Russo, it escalated into something more serious and eventually led to competition.

Since winning the 2002 Vermont Golden Gloves title and the New England Golden Gloves Novice Championship, Lisa has posted an impressive list of boxing accomplishments–the 2006 Ringside World Champion, 2006 and 2007 U.S. National Champion, 2006 and 2007 Golden Gloves National Champion, and the 2006 Bronze Medalist-Pan Am Games in Buenos Aires, Argentina. Lisa also boxed in the 2006 Women's World Amateur Championships in New Delhi, India, and was Captain of the 2006 U.S. Elite Women's Boxing Team, while being ranked #1 in the USA at 145 pounds. She has also won numerous Northeastern Regional Championships, and was the 2007 New England Golden Gloves "open class" Champion. Where can we find Lisa–where else but the Portland [Maine] Boxing Club!

Lisa has come a long way in a short period of time since winning her first career bout in Burlington's Memorial Auditorium in 2002. Lisa stands nearly six feet tall, and uses her height and reach to her advantage. The welterweight bout with Theresa Brown, of the Green Mountain Boxing Club out of Rutland, was stopped in the third round after Kuronya repeatedly inflicted damage with a strong jab. She advanced to the New England Golden Gloves Novice Championship where Lisa earned a split decision over Gina Klay.

In the open class welterweight division at the 2007 New England Golden Gloves Tournament of Champions, Lisa won an unanimous decision over Margaret (Perry) Morgan out of Murphy's gym in Manchester, New Hampshire.

Lisa has literally traveled throughout the United States and the world participating in club shows and tournaments. In the 2007 USA Boxing National Championships, Lisa decisioned Nicole Woods of Stone Mountain, Georgia, in the semi-finals. She went on to stop Brittany Inkrote of Red Lion, Pennsylvania in the finals for the championship. Lisa had previously defeated Nicole Woods in the semi-finals, and decisioned Stephanie Taylor in the 2006 finals.

In the 2006 Women's World Amateur Boxing Championships in New Delhi, India, Lisa would lose to the reigning World Champion, Canada's Mary Spencer [Windsor, Ontario]. Likewise, Spencer would again defeat Lisa at the 2006 Pan Am Championships, but brought home a bronze medal.

Lisa would go on to win at the 2006 and 2007 National Golden Gloves Championships, once again defeating Nicole Woods. Liz Leddy, also of the Portland Boxing Club, came up against a strong Caroline Barry of Colorado.

Lisa's biggest influence was from her coach, Bobby Russo, "His passion for boxing and generosity to develop his boxers is priceless," she recalled. Though in all fairness, Lisa is a very dedicated boxer and puts in a lot of hard work while working a full-time job as an environmental scientist.

For Lisa boxing has been one of the most challenging and rewarding activities–involving strength, agility, discipline, motivation, balance, coordination and a competitive mentality.

Overcoming gender differences and discrimination has been a task for Lisa though. In the future, she hopes to continue to advance to nationally recognized tournaments, while helping to make it easier and more acceptable for women to box in the years to come. She would also like to assist coach Bobby Russo in training more women for competition.

A native of Bethlehem, Pennsylvania, Lisa graduated from West Chester University, but now makes her home in Portland, Maine.

Chapter Five

The Golden Gloves in Vermont

The Vermont Golden Gloves
By: Michael M. McSorley, Jr.

In the fall of 1991, I left my hometown of Pittsburgh, Pennyslvania, and headed north to start college at Saint Michael's College in Winooski, Vermont. I didn't know anyone there, but quickly became friends with a group of characters from Boston and NYC. Most of them were also Irish Catholic and we all had similar interests: girls, partying, hockey and skiing. Having played high school hockey in Pittsburgh, I considered going out for St. Mike's team, but decided against it after realizing my New England classmates had competed at a much higher prep school and elite travel levels. Without hockey to look forward to, I promised myself that I'd hit the weights harder than ever to stay in shape. Unfortunately at that time, St. Mike's weight room was closed for the construction of their new student recreation center. Searching for other work out alternatives, I ran down the hill from St. Mike's into the town of Winooski.

In Winooski, I spotted a World's Gym. I walked in and saw state of the art dumbbells and machinery. Men and women were working out in the latest cheesy spandex apparel. Most of the walls in this place were covered with contest photos of the gym's owner Mario, who looked to be over 60. When I inquired about membership costs, the girl behind the counter gave my tattered t-shirt, shoes and shorts a once over followed by a condescending sigh and eye roll. Their monthly rate was way too expensive for my Natural Lite Beer and Rahmen Noodle college budget. As I ran back up the hill to St. Mike's, I came across a flyer stapled to a telephone pole. It read "Moriarity's Gym, Kickboxing and Boxing, Beginners Welcome, College Discount". The next day some hockey players and I ran down to Malletts Bay Avenue to check out Moriarity's. The windows out front were so steamed up you couldn't see through. Inside, the gym was nothing more than a mid sized room that probably once served as a neighborhood storefront. There were two heavy bags, a double end bag, a speed bag, a round by round timer, some wall mirrors, and a carpeted floor. The owner, Joe Moriarity, was a tough beefy guy from Boston with powerful legs the size of tree trunks. I'd guess that he was about 33 years old. Joe took us under his wing and showed us some boxing basics. Within 3 workouts, he had us in headgear sparring each other and eventually him. The gym didn't have a ring and the carpeted floor provided minimal cushioning when we slipped or got knocked down. Joe generally took it easy on us, but would occasionally spin and rip a round house back kick, purposely missing our face by inches. At that time, Joe was training for a toughman contest across the lake in Plattsburgh, New York. If we got sloppy and dropped our guard, he'd make us pay by giving us a head or body shot. One body shot knocked the wind out of me and I took a knee. "Get Up, Your OK! C'Mon Mike," he shouted. Sometimes when we'd land a hard clean shot on Joe ... he'd just laugh. As nice a guy as Joe was, he was equally intimidating.

Within a month, Joe asked me if I'd be interested in competing in the local Golden Gloves. Truthfully, I was scared of the idea and didn't think I was ready. "Joe, what if they put me in against a really experienced guy?" I asked. "I won't let them ...." he replied. "Besides, I won't even let you in there unless I think you've trained hard and your ready. Don't worry ... I'll get you some good sparring. I don't want you going in there getting your ass kicked or getting hurt. I won't let that happen. I won't let anyone represent my gym unless they are ready!"

Joe was a good salesman and gave me no reason not to enter the tournament. I knew that he was true to his word about getting me ready. At that time, I was just getting settled at college. I was making new friends, chasing girls and trying to get into the pubs with my fake ID from West Virginia. Hard core training for the Golden Gloves wasn't a realistic option for me.

By my sophomore year at St. Mike's, I went to Moriarity's less and less. My grades were seriously suffering and I was enjoying the Burlington night life a little too much. The few times that I did jog down to Moriarity's, Joe seemed pissed at me for my lack of commitment. Before I knew it, my sophomore year had come and gone. I had nothing to show for that year except a small beer gut and bad grades. My parents weren't pleased. That summer back in Pittsburgh, I decided to hit the weights hard. When I returned to Winooski in the fall for my junior year, I weighed in at a beefed up 220 lbs. I was as strong as I've ever been, but I felt stiff and unathletic. That first week back, I jogged down to Moriarity's and found a FOR RENT sign in the window. I heard a rumor that Joe headed back to Boston. By November, I decided I needed a goal. Something to train for. I decided to give the Golden Gloves a go at light heavyweight. It would mean that I had to drop 45 lbs AND find a place to train. My roommate Minny (a natural middleweight) also decided to enter. I went home to Pittsburgh for Thanksgiving and knew it would be my last time to eat well before the Gloves in late January.

I started dropping water weight pretty fast. Getting down to 195 wasn't too tough. Getting below that was a different story. I realized that alcohol and booze were my worst enemies due to all of the empty calories. I started bartending at the Blarney Stone Pub on St. Paul Street in Burlington and gave up drinking. The Blarney Stone's owner was a fun loving, gregarious guy named Brian. Brian let me work extra shifts, which helped with the temptation of getting on the other side of the bar. Within a month, Brian's older brother Craig also started working at the pub. Craig was the most laid back guy you could ever meet. He was your All-American clean cut intelligent guy. He also had extensive training in Ju-Jitsu and Aikido. After getting to know him, I asked him if he help me train for the gloves and he agreed. Craig put a heavy bag in his garage and put a small gas heater in there to combat the freezing temperatures. In addition to some light sparring with Craig, I sparred some of my classmates in a garage on East Street in Winooski.

A buddy of mine who played on the baseball team introduced me to the team's pitcher named Jake Mosher. Jake was also a junior at St. Mike's and he was a native Vermonter. In addition to baseball, he had an extensive successful kickboxing record. Jake also was training for the gloves and was going to compete at welterweight. Like myself, Jake was an English major. His father, Howard Frank Mosher, was an accomplished author (which Jake would also later become). Without question, Jake was the most intense and focused guy that I have ever met. On weekends, he headed north to his hometown of Irasburg, Vermont, where he was an expert hunter and fisherman. Jake, Minny and I sparred a few times in a dingy, freezing empty garage on East Street in Winooski. Despite my height, weight, and reach advantage, Jake was an excellent sparring partner. He had quick hand speed and good foot work. Two things that I needed to work on. During our sparring, he worked on slipping my jab and going to the body.

The Golden Gloves tourney loomed in the distance. January was only two months away. I was stuck at 190 lbs and drove 12 hours home to Pittsburgh for St. Mike's 4 week Christmas break. Most of the boxing gyms in Pittsburgh were in the ghetto. I trained at Jack's Uptown Gym in the Hill District and Hogan's gym downtown. At both places, I was in the minority as a white fighter. Junior, the father of a close friend of mine, owned the building where Jack's was located. Junior was the Pittsburgh boss of the Genovese family. He didn't charge the gyms manager, an old black man known as Big Jack, any rent. It was also free for fighters to train there. Junior's daughter told me that her Dad saw the place as a way to give back to the community. He was an old school Pittsburgh Italian guy and he had no tolerance for drugs or bullshit. His business was strictly the lucrative numbers racket that thrives in the rougher sections of town. I never saw Junior at the gym while I trained there. The heroin pushers, hookers, and junkies never hung out in front of Jack's Uptown Gym out of fear and respect. Instead, they stood on the adjacent corner in front of a shady run down bar called Red's. It was intimidating walking out to my car in the dark after each workout. I always looked over my shoulder when I left Jack's.

The walls of Jack's were adorned with old area fight posters and boxer's pictures. One vintage photo had Hall of Fame light heavyweight Billy Conn hitting the heavy bag. Billy Conn had lived in my neighborhood (Squirrel Hill) and was considered a legend. Many consider him to be the best light heavyweight ever. During my junior year in high school, a story about Billy appeared all across the local and national news. One morning after church, the then 72 year old Conn and his beautiful wife, Mary Louise, stopped for coffee at a neighborhood convenience store. A young robber entered the store, walked past the Conns, demanded money from the cashier and threatened to pull out his gun. The cashier challenged the robber to show the weapon and the robber leaned over and grabbed cash from the register. A struggle ensued and Billy stepped in, punched the robber, knocking him to the floor. He proceeded to try to hold the robber for the police, but he got away running down the street with $80 from the register. The robber left one of his shoes and a sweatshirt on the floor of the store from the scuffle. After hearing the news, all of my classmates and I at nearby Central Catholic thought he was the coolest old man. My grandparents and their generation will always remember his classic 1941 heavyweight battle against Joe Lewis.

The other Pittsburgh gym that I trained at was Hogan's. Hogan's was smack dab in the middle of downtown Pittsburgh in the basement of an old office building. Many of the region's top amateurs and pros trained here (including future IBF lightweight champion Paul Spadafora, currently 40-0). The problem I faced at both gyms was that none of the trainers wanted to invest any time in a fighter who was preparing to fight in Vermont. If they weren't going to be in your corner, they weren't interested. Despite this, I went to the gyms every day over Christmas break and soaked in as much as I could. The more I went, the more people were willing to give me pointers. Respect is earned, not freely given out at any boxing gym.

When I returned to Winooski after the break, I had received the Vermont Golden Gloves application from long time director Ernie Farrar. Since I didn't have a real gym to train at, I called Farrar up and asked him for any suggestions. He was kind enough to put me in touch with a St. Mike's graduate who lived in the area named Mike Armstrong. Armstrong was a middle aged successful real estate salesman. He was solid boxer during his college days at St. Mike's and stayed involved with the sport by being a referee every year in the Vermont Golden Gloves. Minny and I headed over to Armstrong's Colchester house to meet him and train. He had a beautiful home with a full ring in the basement. Action photos of Marvelous Marvin Hagler were on the walls. Armstrong's basement gym was much more spacious and nicer than Moriarity's or either of the Pittsburgh gyms. Before Armstrong even let us inside his house, he made it clear that he could not train us due to the conflict of interest of his tournament referee duties. He also told us that he would not ref any of our fights. He was a hard nosed, no nonsense guy and made little eye contact with Minny and I. He made us feel that our brief meeting with him was a tremendous inconvenience for him. None the less, Minny and I were very grateful and respectful of his time. That night, Mike let us practice our footwork in the ring and he gave us some pointers. He told us–" Don't be scared if you get in the ring and see your opponent is some tough looking guy with a busted up crooked nose .... it probably means he has no defense ... Be scared if your opponent has a perfect record and a straight nose!"

Before we left that night, Armstrong told us he scheduled for Minny and I to meet with boxing trainer Ed Patterson way out in Duxbury, Vermont. We really appreciated him doing this for us. When we arrived at Ed's place, it was very dark outside and there were no street lights around. Right next to his spacious home was a barn. I can't quite recall, but I believe his boxing gym was in a refinished section of the barn. It was a well equipped gym with a small ring and it had all the essentials. Ed was a likeable guy who had tremendous patience with Minny and I. He volunteered to work our corner and Craig served as his assistant corner man. We trained at Patterson's place for the two remaining weeks before the fights. It was late in the game, but better late than never. Minny and I felt a tremendous relief having Ed and Craig working our corners. One night on the drive out to Waitsfield, Craig stressed the importance of staying away from women before the fight. "It'll get you focused and mean," he told us. I had just started dating a pretty freshman, so I took his advice and kept my distance. In fact, I asked her to not even attend the fights out of fear that I would lose.

Finally, the big day arrived. It was a typical frigid, snowy Vermont January day. Minny went down to the auditorium early and made his 156 limit with ease. I headed down later, stripped down to my boxer shorts, hopped on the scale and came in at 176. Those final 3 weeks of dieting were really a bitch and I felt pretty weak, but making weight was a huge relief. The state mandated tournament physician checked all of the fighters. When he got to me, everything checked out OK, except for one question he asked: "Do you wear contact lenses or glasses?" "Contacts," I told him. "Your gonna have to take them out before your fight," he said. I told him that I would, but I lied. Without my contacts I was blind as a bat. Besides, I only had them knocked out a few times while sparring. I was ready to take my chances. That afternoon, a Fed-Ex package arrived at my apartment. One of my classmate's father sent me a white and green silk boxing robe. His Dad grew up in the Bronx and fought in the Golden Gloves as a kid. He became a successful oil broker and still had friends in the fight game. He picked up the robe at the NYC's famous Gleason's Gym and had it overnighted for my fight. It really was thoughtful and a great surprise.

That night, a ton of our friends and classmates showed up for the fights and the auditorium was beginning to get packed. Just before I warmed up backstage with Craig and Ed, a short muscular fighter from New Hampshire sized me up in the hallway. He had a diamond studded lightning bolt earring, a large panther tattoo on his arm, and a few lines shaved into the side of his hairdo.

"Where you from cuz?" he quipped.

"St. Michael's College just up the road, where are you from?" I replied.

"Dude ... I go to the school of hard knocks," he said.

Before long, this little welterweight wiggerish tough guy was in the ring. His opponent was a tall, pale skinny, gangly French Canadian kid from Montreal. By the initial looks of it, I thought the French Canadian was going to get slaughtered. As they touched gloves before the opening bell, the wigger stared up at the Frenchman and gave him a menacing smirk. The bell rang and the wigger came out of his corner throwing bombs. His only problem was that none of them were landing. The Frenchman hardly threw any punches. Instead, he bobbed and weaved and ducked everything that came his way. At the end of the round, the wigger walked back to his corner looking exhausted. He was very slow getting off his stool for the start of the 2'd round. The French Canadian kid picked up the pace and came right at him. With the wigger barely able to keep up his tired arms to defend himself, the French Canadian utilized his reach advantage to pick him apart and scored a TKO victory.

Minny was up next at middleweight. His opponent was a high school senior from South Burlington. The second the bell rang, his opponent ran across the ring and caught Minny flush with a wild looping overhand right. It knocked Minny off of his feet into the ropes, and almost completely out of the ring. The crowd went nuts! Minny jumped right up and was visibly furious and red faced. He immediately started for his opponent but the ref held him back and proceeded to deliver a standing 8 count. When the count was up, Minny raced at the kid and they each stood toe to toe blasting each other with hooks until the bell. The 2nd round, Minny jumped on him and hit him with a bunch of hard blows.

The kid fell into the ropes covering up and the ref delivered a standing 8 count. When the count was up, Minny continued to pounce on him and hit him with a left hook that again dropped him into the lower ropes. Seeing that the kid was too wobbly to get up, the ref immediately called the fight. Minny raised his arms triumphantly and the crowd was rocking after this see-saw battle.

There were two light heavyweight fights before mine and all of the fighters looked good. I ended up fighting a kid named Jim Evans from Glover, Vermont. We both had the same build and both had zero Golden Glove experience. We both threw boxing technique out of the window and hurled haymakers at one another. Between each round Ed spoke calmly and firmly getting my attention. He gave very specific pointers and held my face and made me look right into my eyes as he spoke.

"ONE–Keep your left guard up at all times."

"TWO–When you throw the right, follow it up with your jab while stepping back."

"THREE–Breathe deep through your nose and calm down. You are winning the fight."

Ed knew that my adrenaline was pumping. His ringside experience and slow emphatic points got my attention. I landed just a few more shots and won the fight by decision. Minny and I were thrilled to advance to the semi finals!

The following week, I really struggled to make weight. I noticed that Minny didn't seem to be dieting and he didn't join me to train at Ed's gym. He didn't seem to be himself, the day of the semi-finals he disappeared. I contacted his girlfriend and she panicked. Since his motorcycle was also missing, she worried that he might have been in an accident. I went down to the auditiorium and tournament officials confirmed that he hadn't weighed in yet. I weighed in at 178lbs. The whole Minny MIA situation weighed heavily on my mind as I sat in the auditorium dressing room waiting for my fight. Ed walked in, set down his corner man ice bucket and said: "Cut off your wraps and pack up your stuff. Your opponent cancelled due to injury. You get a bye win. Congratulations, your fighting next week for the state championship! .... Don't celebrate just yet though ... we have a lot of work to do this week!"

I sat in the bleachers and felt emotionally drained from the events of the day. I sat and watched Jake Mosher win his welterweight bout and also advance to the finals. My opponent for the championship was decided by the winner of that night's other light heavyweight fight. Saratoga Springs, New York's Gary Wilcox fought the defending champion Steve Keach from Biddeford, Maine. Both fighters were in great shape and they proceeded to pound one another for three rounds. Keach won, but it could have gone either way. A year after the fight, Wilcox turned pro and is currently 20-3 campaigning at heavyweight. I knew that I had my work cut out for me in the Championship against Keach. He was a hard puncher.

When I got home that night, Minny was playing solitaire at the kitchen table. He never looked up from the cards and he seemed bummed out. Seeing him made me feel relieved and pissed all at once. He apologized for not letting me know where he was and he told me he felt like he pulled a muscle in his stomach after that Vermont fight. He also mentioned that he thought his competition looked too strong. I felt bad for him. He was a good friend, and a solid guy. Communication wasn't always one of his finer points, but we all have our peccadillos.

That week Craig and I made the 45 minute drive to Duxbury in snowstorms. During those drives, Craig stressed the importance of keeping my focus and sticking with a game plan. Craig and Ed had me work on my jab and movement. He wanted me to focus on when Keach would plant his feet. They'd stress: "When you see him plant his feet, stick out the jab and step to the right to get out of the way and come back with a right counter." Keach was a power puncher, but he often attacked with his guard open. That week was the slowest of my life. All I could think about was the fight.

When the Championship day arrived, I drove to the auditorium in a blizzard and weighed in at 180lbs. They grant you a 2 lb overage, so I was right on the money. As I left the auditorium, I walked past a short muscularly ripped black boxer skipping rope in a rubber suit. I realized that it was the guy that Minny was supposed to fight the week before. The snap of his jump rope echoed throughout the empty auditorium. Had I weighed one more pound, I would have had to do the same thing. I went home and slept and relaxed. My phone rang constantly, but I never answered. Friends, family, and even St. Mike's alumni that I hardly knew left messages wishing me luck. I eventually headed down to the auditorium and stretched out. An old cutman offered to tape up my hands. He wrapped them up perfectly. They felt heavy and hard, like two mallets.

There was a heavy snowstonn outside and Craig and Ed hadn't arrived yet. I decided to sit out in the bleachers to watch the first fights. Mike Armstrong walked over and sat next to me but looked straight ahead. He said: "Don't talk, don't even look at me. Just stare at the ring and listen to me. You got lucky to be here tonight. Your fighting the defending champ tonight, not some inexperienced farm hand like two weeks ago. Your not going to beat this kid. He's has more fights, more experience and he's a harder puncher than you. Go out there and do what Ed told you, don't make this into another street fight!"

Just then, some drunk bearded wombat sitting behind us leaned forward and pointed at me. He yelled: "Hey ref, I got a *?!* question for you. Are you reffin' this kid's fight?"

Armstrong spun around and snapped "No ... I'm not. Mind your own business!" he then walked away quickly. The guy then looked down at me and said "It IS my business if your talking to him and he's reffin your fight tonight!!" "Don't worry!" I said "He's not reffin' my fight! There's no *?!* conspiracy here!" I stormed off back to the dressing room pissed at the world. I was pissed about Armstrong's comments. I was pissed at that nosy wombat in the bleachers. I was pissed about the blizzard outside and worried that Craig and Ed hadn't arrived yet! About 10 minutes before showtime, Ed and Craig walked in.

The auditorium was packed and my Dad even flew up from Pittsburgh for the championship fight. He ended up randomly sitting next to Jake Mosher's folks. Two fights before mine, Jake fought a tough kid from Bellow Falls, Vermont, via way of the Virgin Islands named Marcos Nieves. Nieves had fought for one year and trained at the Granite State Boxing Club. Despite Nieve's reach advantage, Mosher fought a very tough fight the first 2 rounds. Towards the end of the 3rd, Jake charged and walked into a hard jab–right cross combo that sent him down to the canvas hard. The KO sent the doctor into the ring. Fortunately, Jake was OK. Nieves was a class act and walked over to check on him as he laid there surrounded by the doctor and his corner people. Jake got helped up to his feet and left the ring on his own. He was a very tough kid and had nothing to be ashamed of He undoubtedly gave it his all. It just wasn't his night.

Next up was a brutal middleweight bout between a tough rolly poly French Canadian named Marcel Aubut and a ripped experienced boxer named Adrian Brown. After three rounds of non stop action, Marcel Aubut won a narrow decision. That fight was tough for anyone to follow. The crowd was still giving both fighters a standing ovation as I entered the ring. For the championship fights, the ring announcer gave longer introductions to each fighter and they even had play by play local TV commentators at ringside. I wore a white tank top that my mom sent up with my Dad that read IRISH in green lettering across the chest. As I entered the ring, the obnoxious drunk wombat from earlier screamed:

"We'll see how IRISH you are!"

I stared out of the ring at him and my blood boiled. I then focused across the ring at Keach. At the opening bell, Keach rushed me and caught me with a good hook to the body and head. For the first two minutes, we stood in the middle of the ring and exchanged blows. I heard Craig screaming " Jab ... Jab" from my corner. Unwisely, I had abandoned my game plan. Keach walked into a hard hook to the chin that doubled him over. For a second I thought I had him in trouble, but he kept coming. He then landed a shot to my head that send both of my contacts lenses airborne. With my nose badly bleeding, the ref gave me a standing 8 count. With seconds left in the round, he continued his attack near the ropes. He threw about six consecutive punches and then the ref then jumped in and stopped it. I was surprised at the early stoppage. For a second, I bitched to the ref that I was fine to go on, but he shook his head and told me I was bleeding too much. I glanced down and saw that my tank top was splattered with blood. Ed cleaned up my nose and then I headed to the center of the ring. The decision was announced and Keach's arm was raised in victory.

I headed to the dressing room to shower and saw Keach in the hall. I wished him good luck in the New England championships and he thanked me. My Dad told me he was proud of me. My Dad, Craig and I headed down to the Blarney Stone. The pub was rockin' and the tournament was finally over. Although I didn't win the state title, I gained memories to last a lifetime. Along the way I met a lot of great people and some real characters. Despite the first round TKO loss, we celebrated as though I had won. The beer and wings never tasted so good.

Saint Michael's College, Michael McSorley, being introduced to Burlington Memorial Auditorium in the championship.

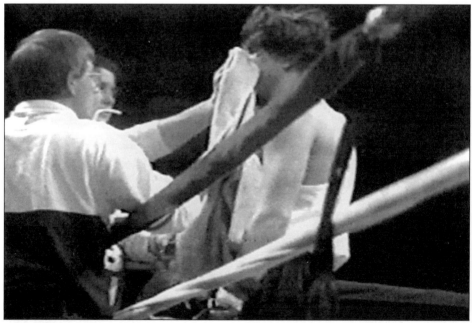

After suffering a first round TKO loss, Mike McSorley gets his nose attended to by trainers Ed Patterson and Craig Bernedette.

Golden Gloves History

The name "Golden Gloves" was born in 1923 when a Chicago sports editor, Arch Ward, originated a boxing tournament designed to help youth and promote amateur competition.

The tournament's sole material award was a tiny golden glove, symbol of the amateur championship, which went to the winner of each weight division. Thus, the name "Golden Gloves" took on significance and the tournament was so titled.

The first Golden Gloves tournament was held in 1923 in the Chicago Stadium under the sponsorship of the Chicago Tribune, whose sports editor, Ward, conceived the idea. The tournament was tremendously popular and the idea of a big amateur boxing show was launched successfully.

A second Golden Gloves tournament was not held until 1928, however, because of legal technicalities. Boxing was legalized in Illinois that year. Then the tournament was revived, with the Chicago Tribune and the New York Daily News beginning the first of yearly amateur shows. In the early days, tournaments were for local boys only but soon requests poured in from boys in other cities who wanted to compete.

Newspapers in other cities were asked to cooperate in promotion of tournaments in their areas and to bring their champions to Chicago and New York to box other winners in super-tournaments.

Heretofore, the New York Daily News held a tournament of champions for eastern Seaboard cities. Chicago, under the Tribunes direction did so for other sections of the country. Champions of each tournament met annually, alternately in Chicago and New York, to determine national Golden Gloves championships. Under the present organization, only one Tournament of Champions is held. A new tournament site is selected annually.

The Golden Gloves program for the United States is organized on a territorial basis to give all sections of the country representation. New York conducts their own tournament.

All tournaments are planned, promoted and directed without outside interference, within limits of the amateur code, and in keeping with Golden Gloves' high purpose and ideals. The same is true for all the feeder tournaments such as the Vermont Golden Gloves.

What Is a Golden Glover?
by Lou Winston

He may be the only child or have five sisters and/or two brothers. A Golden Glover may be a little fellow of 4'9" or a giant of 6'5".

He may be a tender 18 year old of 250 pounds, or a jockey size matured young man of 26.

He may be gaunt, or lean, but is mostly muscular.

He may be a 6th grade drop-out or a student attending college.

He may be single, a divorcee of 19, or married and a father of six.

He may not smoke or drink, because of the rigid training program required of a Golden Glover.

He may be a boy who travels more than 100 miles five nights a week, merely to train, and may refuse to run an errand of one block for his wife or mother.

He may be a boy who sacrifices pleasure for days, weeks, yes, months of strenuous training just to enter the Golden Gloves and make a good showing.

He may be a plumber or a barber, a machinist or a policeman, a laborer or a cook, a student or a school teacher, he may be unemployed.

He may be rich or of wealthy parents, or have a mediocre income, but usually has difficulty in balancing his books financially.

He may be a son of foreign born parents, but he almost without exception is a United States citizen by birth.

He may be Japanese, Mexican, English, Swedish, Norwegian, Irish, Italian, Polish or Jewish.

He may be from every State in the Union, including Hawaii and Alaska.

He may be negro or white or an Indian, or a mixture of Chinese and American.

He may possess the ambition to become a World's Champion and enter the professional field of boxing, or he may end his career in the Golden Gloves with only one fight.

He may be an ex-serviceman or one to be inducted soon after the close of a Golden Gloves Tournament.

He may be a boy taking his initial airplane flight or be quartered in a hotel for the first time.

He may be a boy separated from home only once, or he may be a restless one who wanders.

He is the type of fellow who expends every ounce of energy in the ring for a medal or trophy, instead of fighting for cash.

He is a young man alone in the ring with his opponent, with no one to run interference for him and no one to whom to pass the ball when the going gets rough.

He is a youth searching for a rainbow–to see–to touch–to grasp–and to keep.

This–my friends–is a GOLDEN GLOVER.

To student
of
the sweet science.

this school bell

clangs,

calling two,

only two,

to class

in a square roped ring

where they

sweat out

a final exam

in the bobbing and

weaving Philosophies

of Sullivan,

Armstrong,

and Dempsey,

of Marciano,

Robinson,

and Ali,

where each earns

straight A's

for courage,

for character,

for being there.

We salute the Golden Gloves,

its participants, its supporters,

its future.

® MARVEL PRINTING CO.

SINCE 1973

12/22/2006

Hours of Operation:
4:00 pm to 8:00 pm Monday - Friday
Noon to 6:00 pm Saturday
Open Year Round!

BANTAM BOXING
SINCE 1973

Billy Lefebvre
Bantam Boxing Club
88 Mallets Bay Avenue
Winooski, VT 05404

Gym # 802-655-0060
Cell # 802-238-5421
Email: bantam118@yahoo.com
Websites: www.bantamboxing.com
www.myspace.com/bantamboxing

Billy Lefebvre
USA Boxing Certified
Level 2 Coach #2529008027

35 Years of Successful Experience as a
Boxer, Trainer, Coach and Manager!

Amateur and Pro!
FREE Trial Lesson!
$50.00 monthly
includes all training!

Also please visit www.expertvillage.com, the "World's Largest How-To Video Site" to
view our 300 plus videos on "How To Box", search keyword Lefebvre.
We are the ONLY USA Boxing Officially Registered, Certfiied and Insured Training
Facility in the Greater Burlington Area!

Joe Lefebvre
PERSONAL BOXING TRAINER
New England Golden Gloves Champion
3 Time VTGG Champion - 3rd Generation Boxer

Bantam Boxing Club | *Rates starting at*
88 Malletts Bay Ave. | *$10 per hour.*
Winooski, VT 05404 | *References Available!*

Cell # 802-922-6675   Gym # 802-655-0060
Email: vtboxingtrainer@yahoo.com
Website: www.bantamboxing.com

Duane Lefebvre
PERSONAL BOXING TRAINER
3 Time VTGG Champion - 3rd Generation Boxer

Bantam Boxing Club | *Rates starting at*
88 Malletts Bay Ave. | *$10 per hour.*
Winooski, VT 05404 | *References Available!*

Home # 802-899-4421   Gym # 802-655-0060
Email: vtboxingtrainer2@yahoo.com
Website: www.bantamboxing.com

Ernie Farrar (right) presenting Bernie Cummings (left) with an award.

Firpo's Team 1948. Firpo (far left); Harry Perrigo (3rd from Firpo); Guido Tarquino (2nd from right–standing).

Bernie Cummings (right) and young Tony Farrar (left) in early 1980s.

Dr. Richard Bernstein (left) with Unknown Boxer and Ref Al Loukes (right).

Referee Jim Lavoie

1961 Lowell, Massachusetts. L-R: Paul Savage, holding the Rocky Marciano Trophy for the Heavyweight Championship that he had just won. John Cunavalis, Vermont Official. Coach Unknown. Larry Carney, outstanding boxer of the NEGG Tourney holding his trophy.

John Tyrell and Joe Allard. Night of the Fights–Barton Fair Grounds.

Tommy Garrow (left), Ernie Farrar (center) and Billy Kelly (right)

Victor Gammell (left) and Demetrius Andrade (right). 2008 Olympic Boxing Team Member.

Ref Buster Beaupre (far right). 1977 at Burlington Boys' Club.

Jim Churchill (right) at Burlington Boys' Club.

Andrew Jordon (right) and Jimmy Sheridan (left).

The book brought back some memories of when I covered the Golden Gloves for the Burlington Free Press. The stories about Mike Armstrong and Tony Robitaille were especially interesting since I saw both fight successfully at the Memorial Auditorium. There was a lot of work that went into this historical book on boxing in Vermont. If you like boxing and Vermont history, you'll love this book. And while you are reading, take a minute to thank Ernie Farrar for saving Golden Gloves boxing in Vermont. The tournament hosts boxers from Vermont, New Hampshire, Maine and New York. Alan Rubel and Farrar have done a great job. This is good reading for boxing fans. I may even read it twice.

Donald Fillion
Past Sportswriter of Burlington Free Press

Congratulations to Ernie Farrar and Alan Rubel for putting forward the book, "Gloves", the story of Vermont's Greatest Boxers and Personalities "...a record of Boxing in Vermont from its inception in the 1930s on. It started long before I came to Vermont in the early 50s, a history that would be lost if not published.

I particularly enjoyed the years when I was associated with the Golden Gloves with such names as Bernie Cummings, Bobby Lefebvre, Buster Beaupre, Allen Shangraw, Tommy Garrow, Cowboy Lewis, Paul Savage, Donato Paduano and countless others who graced the ring at Burlington Memorial Auditorium, and I'm sorry if I left some other great names out ... it was not intentional. There are some fine vintage photographs of some excellent fighters that were most interesting to persue ... It's a fun read and so very worthwhile, so I was delighted.

It's a lot of fun running back through the years with Ernie and Alan; they deserve a lot of credit for all the research they have done and the countless hours of putting the book together ... As one who covered Golden Gloves for WCAX radio (Blow by blow and ringside announcer and later on with WCAX-TV. I am just delighted that Ernie and Alan put together this history ... Long overdue and well done.

Tony Adams
Retired Sportscaster WCAX-TV

Although I have not been involved in the boxing scene in Vermont, I found "Gloves" riveting by the accounts and stories of pugilism in Vermont over the last Century. In the context of ethnic struggle, long hard winters, and the lure of human competition, the stories of competitors and personalities, many with colorful names and histories, come alive on the page. Weaving together these largely untold slices of human drama, is a major victory and labor of love by Farrar and Rubel. "Gloves" is a must read for anyone taken by this largely invisible piece of Vermont history.

Con Hogan
Author

The Authors

Alan Rubel is a Barre, Vermont, businessman who is currently President of Proforma Vision of Success. A company that does printing, promotional products and E-Commerce. He was past owner of Rubel Home Decorating Center for over 20 years in the City of Barre, Vermont. He was a former Alderman in Barre City and School Board Member in Barre Town. He was selected by the State of Vermont Jaycees as Vermont's Outstanding Young Man for his involvement with his community, youth development and working with the elderly.

Alan Rubel

He has been a guest speaker and past president of his synagogue.

A boxing enthusiast who in 1965 fought in the Vermont Golden Gloves and lost a split decision to Harold Peryea from Altona, New York, and until this day believes he won the fight. "I was robbed!"

Alan E. Rubel

Ernie grew up in Newport, Vermont, graduated from Newport High School, in 1961, worked a year at Ethan Allen Furniture in Orleans. Left the area for Boston in the fall of 1962 to attend school and pursued a career in broadcasting... His first job in radio was at WSNO in Barre and then moved to their sister station, WWSR in St. Albans. He worked mornings for three years and then was hired at WVMT in Burlington where he has been for 41 years. He is currently co-host of the "Charlie and Ernie Show", with

The "Legends" Tony Adams (left) and Ernie Farrar (right).

Charlie Papillo. Tune in some morning, where you'll find plenty of wake up fun! 6-10 am on News-Talk 620 WVMT, Burlington.

Throughout his lengthy broadcast career he has received numerous awards. As producer and host of WVMT's, long running, auto racing show "The Inside Groove", which was billed as "The Fastest Half Hour on Radio" he won three national awards as judged by the journalism department at University of California Irvine. In 1999, he was inducted into the Vermont Association of Broadcasters Hall of Fame. In 2007, he received the prestigious "Ralph Lapoint" award from the Vermont Sportswriters and Sportscasters Association. The Lapoint award comes from nominations solicited statewide from community members. This is one of Vermont's top awards presented annually to people who have shaped the athletic scene in the state through the years. Also in 2007, a resolution was read on the floor of the Vermont House of Representatives commemorating his 40 years of broadcasting at WVMT radio.

In his spare time, he has served on various boards and committees. Involved in Scouting, served on the committee and later assistant Scoutmaster of Troop #1, St. Albans sponsored by American Legion Post #1. Very proud of his oldest son, Tony, who became an Eagle Scout at an early age. Served on the board of directors of the Sportsman's Club of Franklin County for 20 plus years. A certified Vermont Fish and Wildlife Hunter Safety instructor for 15 years and also served on the Vermont Maple Festival committee. He is also Worshipful Past Master of Franklin Lodge #4 F & AM and received his 25 year pin in 2006. Oh yes, he is also a certified official with USA Boxing, the sanctioning body of amateur boxing in the United States.

Ernie is a U.S. Navy veteran, having completed 20 years of service through the U.S. Naval Reserves. He is also a member of the Fleet Reserve Assoc.

Attended Radio Engineering Institute in Sarasota, Florida, and holds an FCC Radio Telephone First Class license. He is also an Amateur Radio Operator (Ham) and holds an Extra Class License with the call sign: WIEF.

Always liked amateur boxing, as it was a way to get youngsters off the streets, give them direction, and show their talent in the ring. In the early 1970's, he worked with Jimmy Sheridan, trainer/coach of the then Franklin County Boxing Club. The club later became the Tri-Town Boxing Club. Through Jimmy's direction Ernie helped organize club shows or the more common name of "Smokers". In 1976, Ernie was asked by George McGuane the Lowell Sun Newspaper if he would or could revive the Vermont Golden Gloves Tournament, which had been dormant for various reasons. He accepted the challenge and as one would say the rest is history. Ernie has been tournament director for the past 31 years. Throughout the year he helps Vermont and New Hampshire boxing clubs organize events to keep the boxers busy and gain more ring experience.

Ernie loves camping and the game of golf, but he will tell you he is probably the worst golfer to step on a course. As luck would have it, he did score a hole-in-one at Arrowhead Golf Course in Milton in 2005.

He is married to the former Sherry Alexander, of North Haverhill, New Hampshire, and between them have 5 children, 9 grandchildren and a great granddaughter, Haven.

In radio circles Ernie is known as the "Dean" of Vermont Radio Broadcasters!

Ernie Farrar

Bob Winkler has worked at the University of Vermont since 1986, and is currently part-time faculty at both UVM and Johnson State College. He created and has maintained the Vermont Boxing History & International Pugilist Review website since 1997. Bob is a member of the International Boxing Research Organization, the National Veteran Boxers Association, Ring #44, Buffalo, New York, and an annual sponsor of the International Boxing Hall of Fame Induction weekend, in Canastota, New York.

Bob Winkler

Resources

AAU Program
Barre Daily Times
Berkshire Evening Eagle, The
Berkshire County Eagle, The
Bennington Evening Banner
BoxRec.com
Brattleboro Daily Reformer
Burlington Free Press
Caledonian Record
Daily News
Fighthouse.com
Fitchburg Sentinel
Lewiston Daily Sun
Lowell Sun & Citizen Leader
MaineToday.com
Manchester Union Leader
Marvel Printing Co.
Newport Daily Express
Plattsburgh Press Republican
Portland Boxing Club
Portsmouth Herald
Reno Evening Gassette
Rutland Herald
Saddoboxing.com
Sportraits
St. Albans Messenger
Sweetscience.com
Times-Argus, The
New York Times, The
USABoxing.org
Vermont Sunday News, The
Washington World Newspaper
WomenBoxing.com

Index

Burrows, Tim 134
Burton, "Kid" 31
Bushey, Hubert 104
Bushey, Mel 90
Bushway, Kenneth "Kid" 33
Buster, "Kid" 31, 35

Cain, Nolan, Dr. 55
Camp Pendleton, California 47
Camp Wildwood, New Hampshire 36
Campbell, Don "KO Frisco" 27
Campo, "Kid" 35
Canadian Junior Olympic Champion 110
Canadian Heavyweight Champion 113
Canadian National Team 100
Canastota, New York 51
Carbonneau, Donald 9
Carbonneau, Frank 9
Carlisle, Kitty 14
Carnera, Primo 15
Carney, Larry 185
Carpenter, Tim 86
Carr, David 55
Carrier Dome 134
Cartee, Jesse 5
Cartee, Ken 6
Carter, Victor, Jr. "Bombshell" ("Vic") 5, 7-9
Casavan, Stephanie 108
Caslin, "Young" 31
Catamount School 132
Castilloux, Dave 44
Catskills, New York
Celli, Tony 31
Center, Brian 94
Cerdan, Marcel, Jr. 100
Champlain Valley Exposition (Essex Junction) 5, 13, 36
Chapdelaine, Art 35
Chaples, Allen "Kid" 10, 26-27, 31
Chaples, Bill 27
Charlotte, Vermont 33, 65, 69
Chavez, Julio Cesar 123
Cheney, Edgar 6, 8
Cheney, Irwin 6, 8
Cheney, Leo (Mr. & Mrs.) 8
Chester, Vermont 33
Chicago Stadium 179

Chicago Tribune 179
Chino Valley, Arizona 105
Christakos, Bobby 110
Churchill, Jim 101-105, 116, 140, 188
Churchhill, Family (Wife: Maggie. Children: Christine, Nicolas, Kiley, Aaron, Ebben James, J.J. and Cody) 105
Chun, Chil-Sung 122
Chuvalo, George 113
Cintron, Kermit 124
Cioffi, Armand "Kid" 10
City Hall 19
Claremont, New Hampshire 69, 133
Clark, Devon 135
Clay, Cassius 51, 74, 78
Cleveland Browns 86
Cliff, Jimmy 65
Clinton, Massachusetts 31-32
Clough, K.O. 7
Clune, Jack 2
Cogston, Herb 90
Cohen, Young 34
Coiffi, Kid 34
Cokley, John 51
Colchester, Vermont 5, 34
Coleman, Jim 77
Colombo, Charles 18
Colon, Miguel 148
Colorado Springs, Colorado 145
Colton, Jerry 151
Columbo, Al 71
Commissioner of Boxing 54
Community Hall (Montpelier) 155
Comolli, Dick 16
Comolli, John J. 15
Concurrent Military Training Camp 5 (Colchester), 36 (Winooski)
Conley, Charles (Charlie) 5, 7, 12
Conley, "Young" 31
Conn, Billy 171
Constantino, Dan 135
Continental Football League 85
Conti, Frankie 42
Cook, Sid 34
Cook, "Speed Demon" Kid 31
Cooley, John 94
Coolidge, President Calvin 13

192, 186
Farrar, Tony 184
Fay, "Kid" 13, 31
Feeley, Randy 116
Fields, Dave 98, 109-110
Fighthouse (NYC) 123
Fillion, Don 95
Firpo's Restaurant 15
Firpo-Alywood Boxing Show 7
First Team All American 85
Fitchburg Sentinel 41
Fitz, "Battlin" 10, 34
Fitzgerald, Jim 55
Fitzgerald, Mark 110
Flanagan, "Young" 33
Flowers, Jackie 30, 43
Flying Auger Brothers 10
Flynn, "Young" 32
Flynn, "Irish" Paddy 32
Folks, Johnny 51
Fontaine, Norm 77
Forest, Jimmy 81-83, 93
Forkas, Lou 7-8, 41
Fort Ethan Allen 7-8, 34, 41
Fortin, "Kid" 34
Fournier, Jack (Jackie, "Beebe Bomber") 6-8, 32
Fournier, Roger 35
Francis, Mike 110
Franklin County Boxing Club 56, 191
Franklin County Boxing Team 115
Frederico, George 43
Fuller, Sammy 43
Fusco, Mike 32

Gagner, Ryan 150
Gaignard, Rick 95, 118
Gale, Bob 17, 47, 69
Galendez, Victor 100
Gamache, Joe, Sr. 123
Gamache, Joey 118, 122-124
Gamache, Sissy 124
Gamache, Steve 123
Gamble, "Flash" 35
Gammell, Victor 112-113, 133, 139-142, 187
Gammell, Victor Family (Sarah, Tonya, Sadie) 139

Gardner, Young 35
Garrow, Gary 91
Garrow, Mark 71 (wife: Marie), 107
Garrow, Ralph "Tommy" 68-71, 129-130, 143, 153, 186
Garrow, Ronnie 89-90, 92
Garrow Boxing Club 71
Gates, Perle, 32
Gatti, Arturo 123
Gaudreau 10
Gauthier, Al 18
Gavain, Walter 97
Gelineau, Armand 81, 154-160
General Stark Theatre (Bennington) 14
Gennette, Bob "Pop-Eye" 16, 46-47
Germaine Grenier 91
Germaine, Ted 114
Gero, Howard 90-92
Gibson, Willie 32
Giroux, Jim 130
Gleasons Gym 123, 173
Glenn, Jimmy 124
Glens Falls, New York 13, 91, 102, 112-113, 118, 120-121, 144
Glens Falls Boxing Club 112, 123
Glens Falls Gym 113
Glover, Vermont 7, 174
Gokey, Harold 32
Goldsbury, John 24
Gonzalex, Lester 71
Goodrow, John 77
Goselyn, Narcis 48
Gospel Village 24
Goulette, Young "Iron Man" 3, 30
Grady, Tom 35
Graham, George 98
Grandbois, Josie 148
Grande, Sailor 3
Granger, Joe 82, 91
Granite State Boxing Club 176
Granite Street Hall (Barre) 4-5, 36
Graniteville, Vermont 35, 46, 75
Grant, Gordon 75
Grant, Jimmie 31, 41
Gratton, Henry 114
Graziano, Rocky 56

Wheeler, Ezekiel Dodge 24
White, Bob 85
White, Sailor 34
White Creek, New York 132
Whitehall, New York 89-90
Wilcox, Gary 175
Wildersburgh, Vermont 24
Williams, Clarence 129
Williams, Micky "Kid" 3, 15, 30, 34
Williams, William 24
Williamstown, Vermont 48
Wills, Harry The Black Panther 3
Williston, Vermont 62, 109, 121
Windsor, Ontario
Winkler, Bob 10, 13, 30, 37, 39, 64, 154, 192
Winooski, Vermont 13, 32, 58-59, 73, 77, 79,
    81, 86, 93, 114, 150, 163, 168-171
Winooski National Guard Armory 94, 109
Winooski High School 56, 109
Winooski National Guard Armory 107
Winooski VFW 91-93
Winslow, "Young" 32
Winston, Lou 180
Winter Olympics 78 (Innsbruck, Austria)
    (Grenoble, France)
Women's World Amateur Championships 164-
    165 (New Delhi, India)
Wood, John 94
Woodman Hall (Burlington) 5, 36
Woods, Nicole 165
Woodsville, New Hampshire 31, 35 (Camp
    Wildwood)
Worcester, Massachusetts 14, 17, 31, 33, 43
Worchester, Massachusetts 35, 41
World Amateur Welterweight Champion 146
World Boxing Association-Fedalatin Light
    Heavyweight 138
World Champion 165
World Boxing Council 138
World Boxing Council Continental Americas
    Cruiseweight 138
World Heavyweight Champion 27, 54, 77-78,
    136
World War II 38, 66
World Welterweight Champion 62
World's Gym 168
Wright, Bob 131

Wright, "Wild" Freddie (Bennington's "Rising
    Star") 14, 32
Wright, Jeff 123

Y.M.C.A. (Burlington) 39
Yac, "Battling" 33
Yacavoni, "Big Yack" 27
Yancey, Lloyd 90
Yandow, Bernard 47-48
Yo-Yo Ma 65

Zale, Tony 56
Zelespe, Albert 33
Zider, Father 101